D1238022

Reflections on Human Nature

Reflections

on Human Nature

ARTHUR O. LOVEJOY

The Johns Hopkins Press: Baltimore

This book has been brought to publication with the assistance of
a grant from The Ford Foundation

PREFACE

One of the potential uses of a preface is to explain the title of a book; and at least one word in the present title seems to need some explanation—the word "reflections." The term does not explain whose reflections are in question; but this happens to be a convenient ambiguity, because part of the volume is an attempt at a historical account of the conceptions held—chiefly since the seventeenth and eighteenth centuries—of the desires which motivate human behavior, and of the implications of these theories for economics, politics, and ethics. But the book also contains some observations and critical appraisals by the present author on the same subject, and also some psychological theorems which seem to him unfamiliar and of high importance—namely, the distinction between terminal and adjectival values and the peculiarly complex character of the influence exercised by man's self-consciousness upon his affective and appetitive life. One of the lectures, the third, is wholly devoted to this topic and it manifests itself also in some of the lectures primarily historical in their theme.

The lectures were delivered originally on the Cooper Foundation at Swarthmore College in 1941. I regret the excessive time which because of various circumstances has elapsed between their original deliverance and their present appearance in print. Even after this long interval, the book would hardly have reached publication without the aid of Mr. Bernard R. Mathews, Jr., an advanced graduate student in the department of philosophy at Johns Hopkins University, as research assistant, and his valuable suggestions and discussions with the author.

Arthur O. Lovejoy

Baltimore
July, 1961

CONTENTS

Preface   v

Lecture I   The Self-Appraisal of Man   1

Lecture II   The Theory of Human Nature in the American Constitution and the Method of Counterpoise   37

Lecture III   The Desires of the Self-Conscious Animal   67

Lecture IV   Approbativeness as the Universal, Distinctive, and Dominant Passion of Man   129

Lecture V   The "Love of Praise" as the Indispensable Substitute for "Reason and Virtue" in Seventeenth- and Eighteenth-Century Theories of Human Nature   153

Lecture VI   Approbativeness and "Pride" in Political and Economic Thought   195

Lecture VII   The Indictment of Pride   217

Lecture VIII   Some Ethical Reflections   247

Index   265

Reflections on Human Nature

Lecture I

THE SELF-APPRAISAL OF MAN

The maxim that the knowledge man needs most is knowledge of himself was an article of the religious creed of the Greeks at least two and half millennia ago, and the injunction inscribed upon the temple of Apollo at Delphi has not lacked iteration through the subsequent centuries. But to no generation of men can it have come with more force than to our own. For self-searching is most commonly the offspring of self-distrust and misgivings; it is especially when he feels ill that the plain man becomes curious, and sometimes erudite, about his inward parts. And never before, it is probable, has the reflective portion of mankind suffered a more acute attack of self-distrust or experienced more sudden and disquieting misgivings about its own species. It is the unexpectedness and suddenness of the attack even more than its nature and causes that make our time exceptional. Misgivings of man about himself are nothing new. While his moods, when he thought in general terms about himself at all, have been divided between a tendency to racial self-exaltation and a tendency to a low opinion of himself and of his place in the scheme of things, the latter mood throughout most of Western—not to speak of Eastern—thought has apparently been much the more customary, and certainly the more orthodox; and a thousand religious writers through all ages have seen precisely

1

in man's propensity to self-esteem—to what was usually called "pride"—his chief folly, his primal sin, his gravest danger, and the principal, though by no means the only, reason why he should live in perpetual self-distrust and self-abasement. Of most Western religion, Greek, Hebrew and Christian, the lowering of man in his own eyes, it may on the whole be said, has been the first, though not always the final, concern; and one of the conspicuous historic functions of the belief in God or gods has been to induce in believers, by contrast, a sort of racial inferiority complex, often accompanied by an unpleasantly sycophantic attitude towards deities who themselves, as frequently portrayed, might well have seemed more formidable than admirable.

The examples of this are countless, and many of them trite. But this self-abasement has assuredly been due not solely, perhaps not primarily, to the humbling sense, among the devout, of man's immeasurable inferiority to his God, nor yet, in the theology of Christendom, to the doctrine of original sin; it has often had more empirical and rationalistic grounds, has been the fruit of observation and introspection, of an actual attempt of men to notice what kind of creatures they were, not merely outwardly but inwardly, to generalize these results of observation, and then to appraise their kind by comparing its average or even its universal character and performance with its professed standards, its ideals, or its potentialities. When the Hebrew prophet in the seventh century B.C. observed that "the heart is deceitful above all things, and exceedingly corrupt,"[1] he was uttering

[1] *Jeremiah*, 17:9.

a kind of psychological generalization which may have been already a commonplace, and at any rate remained one for more than two millennia; and the echo of it, and of Augustine, in that monument of Christian doctrine, the Westminster Catechism—"the heart of man is deceitful altogether and desperately wicked"—purported to be evident to the natural understanding even apart from any biblical authority or theological tradition.

Thus Jonathan Edwards shortly before his death, viewing with alarm a tendency which was beginning in the mid-eighteenth century to take a more genial view of human nature, based his refutation of this heresy largely, it is true, upon theological metaphysics and scriptural texts—but also upon more secular considerations. Surveying the course of universal history as he knew it, he concluded that "a view of the successive periods of the past duration of the world, from the beginning to this day, shows that wickedness has . . . had vastly the superiority in the world;" and he offered as his clinching proof the fact that "mankind have been a thousand times as hurtful and destructive as . . . all the noxious beasts, birds, fishes and reptiles in the earth, air, and water put together, at least of all kinds of animals that are visible." "And no creature," Edwards goes on, "can be found anywhere so destructive of its own kind as mankind are. All others for the most part are harmless and peaceable with regard to their own species. . . . Well, therefore, might our blessed Lord say, when sending forth his disciples into the world . . . *Behold I send you forth as sheep in the midst*

of wolves;—BUT BEWARE OF MEN.[2] As much as to say,
I send you forth as sheep among wolves. But why do I
say, wolves? I send you forth into the world of *men*, that
are far more hurtful and pernicious . . . than wolves." If
Edwards could have prophetically extended this survey of
universal history to the twentieth century, it is unlikely that
he would have found reason to change this conclusion.

True, it may be objected that Edwards had a doctrinal
axe to grind, that he looked upon his species with the jaun-
diced eye of a Calvinist. But, except for the quotation—or
misquotation[3]—of Scripture, Edwards was repeating an old
theme of the classical moralists and satirists. That "man is
a wolf to man," *homo homini lupus*, which was a current
cliché in the seventeenth and eighteenth centuries, had been
said by Plautus in the second century B.C., and Pliny and
Juvenal had both declared that no wild animals are so
destructive of their own species as man: "in these days there
is more concord among serpents than among men; wild
beasts are merciful to beasts spotted like themselves. When
did the stronger lion take the life of the weaker? The fierce
Indian tiger lives in perpetual peace with its fellow tigers,
and the wild bear abides in harmony with other bears."[4]

The theme had been more expansively developed—under

[2] *Doctrine of Original Sin Defended; Works*, 1881, II, p. 34.

[3] Luke 10:3, which Edwards is citing, does not say "Beware
of men" or that men in general are *worse* than wolves.

[4] Plautus, *Asinaria*, Act II, sc. lv, line 88: *Lupus est homo
homini, non homo, quom qualis sit non novit.* Juvenal, Satire
XV, 159 ff. For the passage in Pliny, see Lovejoy and Boas,
Primitivism and Related Ideas in Antiquity, p. 402.

the influence, perhaps, both of theological motives and the classical tradition—more than a century before Edwards in a work by a French religious writer which had been translated into English by Sir Philip Sidney and Arthur Goldring:[5]

> What is there more disordered and more contrarie to nature, than is the nature of man himselfe: If beasts of one kind doe kill or eate one another we take it for an ougly thing. What an ouglynesse then ought it to be unto us, when we see how men (who alonly be indued with reason) doe every howre kill one another, and roote out one another: Nay rather, is it not a great wonder to see good agreement and friendship, not among Nations, not between Countries; but even in households, yea and between Chamberfellowes: Wolves are cruell: but yet in what race of wolves shall we find *Caribies* and *Cannibals*? Lyons also are cruell: but yet where were they ever seene in Battell one against another: Now what is warre, but a gathering and packing up together of all the sorts of beastlines that are in the world? And yet what is more common among men than that? . . . It is a playne case, therefore, that man hath made himselfe an underling to the beast.[6]

Essentially this orthodox view of the general badness of

[5] *A Worke concerning the Trewnesse of the Christian Religion . . . by Philip of Mornay*, 1587.

[6] I have omitted other and nontheological examples of the doctrine of "man's essential badness" in the Renaissance; many apposite illustrations of it in that period have now been collected and illuminatingly analyzed by Mr. Hiram Haydn in his *The Counter-Renaissance*, 1950, pp. 405-417.

man was still endorsed, two decades after Edwards, by a writer whom none could suspect of deference to a theological tradition. Voltaire wrote in 1769:

> Men in general are foolish, ungrateful, jealous, covetous of their neighbor's goods; abusing their superiority when they are strong, and tricksters when they are weak. . . . Power is commonly possessed, in States and in families, by those who have the strongest arms, the most resolute minds and the hardest hearts. From which the moralists of all ages have concluded that the human species is of little worth; and in this they have not departed widely from the truth.[7]

The religious writers, at least, usually did not fail to insist that man in his original constitution and his potential supernatural destiny is an admirable creature, made in the image of God; and disquisitions on the "dignity of human nature" were not wholly lacking in conventional works of edification. But in his actual behavior, and still more in his "heart," that is, in his inner affective and appetitive make-up, the springs of action which chiefly move man in his "natural" or unregenerate state, his essential folly and depravity were exhibited as all the more glaring by contrast with what he was meant to be, conceivably might have been, and sometimes supposed himself to be.

It is, then, no new or unusual thing for men to think ill of man, and to have deep misgivings about his nature and his terrestrial prospects; it has been, on the contrary, the dominant strain in men's attitude toward man throughout

---

[7] *Dieu et les hommes*, 1769.

the greater part of history. What differentiates the contemporary phase of this phenomenon from earlier ones is
that it has supervened with an effect of shock upon a period
in which the opposite way of thinking about man had been
becoming dominant. What, in the English-speaking world,
we call the Victorian Era might perhaps best be distinguished
—if one had to choose a single descriptive name for it—as
the Age of Man's Good Conceit of Himself or, in a now
more modish terminology, the Age of Man's Narcissus Complex. The germs of this temper go back, it is true, to an
earlier date in modern history than our historians have always noted; like most things, it had a long and gradual
development. But for a rough historical approximation, we
may date its intensification and its wide diffusion from the
later part of the eighteenth century, when faith in the "perfectibility" of man, and in the consequent inevitability of
continuous (and rapid) progress towards a perfect social
order, began to be preached by powerful spokesmen and to
gain the general ear; and we may see its climax in the
second half of the nineteenth century and the first decade of
the twentieth—though, once more, various beginnings of a
reaction against it may be discerned during the very period
of its triumph. But, in general, it is, I take it, evident beyond the need of argument that in the course of the last
century Western mankind grew steadily more self-com-
placent, more self-confident, and more hopeful about both
the near and the remote future of the race upon this planet.
The belief that man is "naturally good" became a widely
accepted premise alike of politics and pedagogics; the
taste for satire largely went out of fashion in literature, and

the sense of sin rather largely in religion; and to express a "low view" of human nature became a kind of odious blasphemy. Not among the adherents of the Religion of Humanity alone did man receive a sort of self-apotheosis, and his glorification become an article of the creed. A statue of a Victorian statesman bears upon its pedestal the typically Victorian inscription: "Believing in God, he could not lack faith in man"; and amongst those in whom a belief in God was evanescent, faith in man often seemed to take on some of the same practical and emotional functions.

The phases and causes of this more flattering attitude of man towards himself are various, and many of them obvious, though we still lack an adequate historical analysis of it. Such an analysis would, indeed, be a long story, which I shall not attempt here; to do so would result in far too prolix a preamble to my principal theme. Nor is it to my purpose to elaborate upon the diverse aspects and causes of our present disillusionments. The main fact is evident. We all find the spectacle of human behavior in our own time staggering to contemplate; we are all agreed that the world is in a ghastly mess, and that it is a man-made mess; and there is no theme of public discourse now more well worn than the tragic paradox of modern man's amazing advance in knowledge of and power over his physical environment and his complete failure thus far to transform himself into a being fit to be trusted with knowledge and power. The more influential newer tendencies in theology are conspicuously marked by a preoccupation with the reality of evil—of an evil "in the centre of human personality," in Reinhold Niebuhr's words—and by a return to the old emphasis upon the idea of sin.[8] Emerson has become a prophet little congenial to the present dominant mood of mankind.

A generation which has thus been so largely stripped of its late illusions and its too hasty confidence in humanity may naturally be expected to turn to self-examination, and to seek an answer—if it can be had—to the most searching and pressing of all contemporary questions: What is man, and what's the matter with him? If he is to be saved by knowledge, or not without knowledge, it *is,* as the oracle declared, to the knowledge of himself that he must look. For therapeutics is but rarely successful unless preceded by anatomy and pathology. Pure moralizing, ethical theories, the preaching of elevated ideals, have not proved adequate, though they are indispensable, remedies for man's disorders; for we have had many centuries of such preaching and moralizing, and while it has produced some considerable, though local and transient, improvements in human behavior, the total result, when one views the contemporary scene, seems amazingly incommensurate with the ambitions, the magnitude, and the duration of the effort and the genius that have been spent in it. The Christian ethics has been taught for almost two thousand years; the present spectacle of Christendom is, or should be, a profoundly thought-provoking commentary on that fact. The presentation of excellent ideals, in short, has not been lacking; the question is, why they have so little efficacy in shaping the actual life of

[8] For an illuminating survey and critical discussion of these changes, see *The hanging Reputation of Human Nature,* by James Luther Adams, Chicago, 1943.

man. And if we are to find an answer to that question, we shall need a better knowledge of his inner constitution, of the nature, interaction, effects, and relative potency of human motives or springs of action—the emotions and desires that determine men's behavior as individuals and (especially) as groups, since it is as groups, and in particular as political groups, that their behavior is now most atrocious and destructive. Such a knowledge, if or in so far as we had it, might best be called the theory of human nature; it is not yet, I think, sufficiently systematically and penetratingly pursued. It might be expected to be the principal field of inquiry of what is called the science of psychology; yet that discipline, until recently, has had strangely little to say about it. Thirty years ago Leonard Troland began his *The Fundamentals of Human Motivation* with the remark that

> when the layman thinks of psychology, he is usually interested in the nature and interplay of human *motives*. He looks to psychology for some explanation of some peculiarity in the behavior of a fellow man, or in his own desires and impulses. He believes that psychology should tell him why people act as they do, and how their tendencies of action can be modified in desirable directions. . . . [But] anyone who opens a modern text-book of psychology with this interest in mind is doomed to sore disappointment.[9]

And Troland noted as a significant fact that his own book

[9] *Op. cit.*, p. 1.

was apparently the first "to incorporate the word motivation in its title." More recently the late Professor William McDougall could write that, though literature has dealt copiously with "facts of this order, . . . this part of psychology"— which should be "the most important part"—"remains almost ignored by the majority of psychologists."[10] The reason for this—although not, perhaps, the whole reason— McDougall found in "the unfortunate convention which has assigned the study of our intellectual development to the psychologists, and that of our moral development to the ethical philosophers"[11]—who, McDougall perhaps intended to imply, being often bent upon edification, have not usually approached the subject in a sufficiently detached, realistic, and systematic way.

In this respect, however, there has been a notable change within the past two or three decades, a change which Mc-Dougall and Troland, among others, had a part in bringing about. It has owed still more to the influence upon psychologists of the work of certain new schools of psychopathology. The psychiatrist, by the very nature of his calling, is inevitably brought face to face with some of the data most suggestive for the normal psychology of motivation. And about the beginning of the century there appeared, first in Vienna, a group of psychopathologists, led by Freud, who not only propounded new hypotheses about the nature of the subjective determinants explaining abnormal mental states and behavior, but also extended this into a general

[10] *The Energies of Men*, 1933, p. 226, n. 1.
[11] *Ibid.*, p. 233.

theory (in the end, several partially conflicting theories) of human motivation. However incomplete, deficient in scientific caution, and (in some of its details) extravagant Freud's own theory may be considered—with its essentially mythic description of the battles between three metempirical (because "subconscious") entities, the Ego, the Id, and the Super-Ego—it was his great service to have powerfully promoted inquiry into these problems and to have contributed to it some highly original and suggestive conceptions. It must be added, however, that the effect of these recent developments has hardly been to provide man with a more flattering portrait of himself.

2

It is not, however, the purpose of the present lectures to attempt even the sketch of a general theory of human nature, though I hope some essential elements of any such theory may be found in them. They are to be concerned primarily with a portion of the history of the subject. For men—at least the reflective sort of men—have long had theories, though usually rather casual and unsystematic ones, of human nature, its principal springs of action, and the *modus operandi* of volition or deliberate choice. Such theories, implicit if not explicit, can be discerned, if you look for them, in a considerable part of literature, especially in the drama and the novel; in many of the great didactic poems and in some lyric poetry; and, often explicitly, in the writings of theologians, moral philosophers, satirists,

and political theorists. And there are few more important
things to know about a writer than what his express view or
his tacit but controlling assumptions concerning human
nature and its dominant motives were, or to know about a
period than what ideas on these subjects were prevalent in
it. The history of the theory of human nature—of men's
ideas about man—therefore, is, or should be, one of the
major fields of investigation for the student of the history of
ideas. Such a study would seek to ascertain, with respect to
a writing, a school of doctrine, a movement, or a period—
so far as evidence on the matter is available—what type or
types of motive it expressly recognizes or tacitly assumes as
actuating men's behavior, which of them it regards as the
more potent or more usually operative, how it conceives
them to interact with one another, upon which of them the
writers appear to rely, in so far as they themselves aim at
influencing opinion or conduct—and whether, on the whole,
they think well or ill of human nature. With this should be
associated a historical inquiry into the *evaluation* of motives
and of human qualities, or of types of human personality
conceived as the embodiments of such qualities. This last
would be, in great part, a history of men's admirations (or
contempts) of other men, or of the characters portrayed in
fiction; it would include an examination of the fluctuations
of taste in heroes and of the historical conditions under
which these fluctuations took place.

These, patently, are important phenomena in the history
of the human mind, interacting with and often powerfully
influencing other phenomena—most evidently of all political movements and political constitutions. Yet this part of

that history has received little distinct and connected study from intellectual historians, and specialists in the several provinces pertinent to it—i.e., in the history of philosophy, of theology, economics, sociology, politics, and literature— have not, as a rule, been aware of the relations of the particular facts with which their researches are concerned to the theory of human nature as a subject matter common to them all, and needing, for its adequate historical treatment, to be pursued through them all. However, some valuable special studies relevant to parts of it—which is perhaps all that is for the present possible—have of late begun to appear. Mr. Dixon Wecter, for example, has written illuminatingly of *The Hero in American Politics,* Mr. Eric Bentley of the diversities of hero-worship in the past century, and Professor Sidney Hook of *The Hero in History.* But the general notion of such a field of historical study, and an understanding of its problems, is for the most part, so far as I can see, still lacking. We have many works, under various titles, on the history of the idea of God, but none that I can recall on the history of the idea of man. And there is an immense body of learned writing on the changes of taste in literary styles and in other arts, but no comparable investigation of men's changes of taste in human character. The latter is doubtless the more difficult subject, but hardly the less important.

3

Of the history of the theory of human nature these lectures will have to do with one definitely limited chapter. It will be limited both chronologically and topically—to a certain period, and to a certain group of ideas about the dominant and distinctive motives of man which were extremely widely held and especially influential in that period, but were not, of course, the only ones then current. The period is, roughly, the seventeenth and eighteenth centuries. The earlier part of this period was the time in which the unfavorable general appraisal of man may be said to have reached, if not its climax, at any rate its most frequent and most notable expression outside the writings of theologians. The theologians, Protestant and Catholic, continued, of course, to dilate upon the theme; and their writings were probably more copious, and pretty certainly were read by a larger fraction of the public, than in any previous period. But the theme of man's irrationality and especially of his *inner* corruption was no longer a specialty of divines; it became for a time one of the favorite topics of secular literature. For the late seventeenth and early eighteenth centuries were, among other things, the great age of satire; and many of the examples of this genre were by implication, and some of them explicitly, satires on man in general, not merely on peculiar individuals or exceptional types. Boileau's *Eighth Satire* is typical of a number of less familiar examples:

De tous les animaux qui s'élèvent dans l'air,
Qui marchent sur la terre, ou nagent dans la mer,
De Paris au Pérou, du Japon jusqu'au Rome,
Le plus sot animal, à mon avis, c'est l'homme.

Though endowed with reason, he is not at all guided by it, but

. . . dans tout ce qu'il fait n'a ni raison, ni sens.
Tout lui plaît et déplaît, tout le choque et l'oblige,
Sans raison il est gai, sans raison il s'afflige;
Sans raison au hasard aime, évite, poursuit,
Défait, refait, augmente, ôte, élève, détruit.

Exhibiting *homo sapiens* as inferior to the other animals
is one of the customary features of the satires on man.[12]
It was usually admitted that man's reason, if he used it,
would enable him to surpass the other creatures in happiness and in good behavior towards his fellows; but since
he doesn't use it, he "lets instinct better guide the brute."
The principal actual effect of his possession of intellect is
to put him out of harmony with "nature," by engendering
artificial desires and exorbitant ambitions, while increasing
his ridiculousness and fatuity by feeding his vanity. This
general vein of satire, earlier exemplified by Machiavelli
in his *Asino d'Oro*, is continued by La Rochefoucauld, La
Bruyère, Oldham, Mme. Deshoulières, Pope, Swift, Gay,
Francis Fawkes, Robert Gould, the Earl of Rochester, Henry
Brooke, Shenstone, and Goldsmith. Mme. Deshoulières, the
French poetess whom some of her admiring contemporaries
called "the Tenth Muse," in her *Idylle des Moutons* (1692?)
envies the silly sheep, in comparison with man who
proudly boasts of his rationality:

Cette fière Raison dont on fait tant de bruit,
Elle s'oppose à tout, et ne surmonte rien.
   Sous la garde de votre chien
Vous devez beaucoup moins redouter la colère

---

[12] Cf. *The Happy Beast in French Thought of the Seventeenth Century* by George Boas, 1933.

Des loups cruels et ravissans,
Que sous l'autorite d'une telle chimère
Nous ne devons craindre nos sens.[13]

Robert Gould's *Satire on Man* (1708) outdoes Boileau in violence:

What beast beside can we so slavish call
As *Man?* Who yet pretends he's lord of all.
Whoever saw (and all their classes cull)
A dog so snarlish, or a swine so full,
A wolf so rav'nous, or an ass so dull?
Slave to his passions, ev'ry several lust
Whisks him about, as whirlwinds do the dust;
And dust he is, indeed, a senseless clod
That swells, and yet would be believ'd a God.[14]

Gulliver's Travels is, of course, the most elaborate, as it is the most famous, development of this theme. Though usually described as an expression of Swift's own proud, scornful, and bitter temperament, which it is, it is also, especially in the chapter on the Houyhnhnms, an illustration of one of the literary fashions of the time. Its purpose, as summarized by Swift's first editor, Hawkesworth, was the same as that of the writers I have previously quoted: "To mortify pride, which, indeed, was not made for man, and produces not only the most ridiculous follies but the most extensive calamity, appears to have been one general view of the

[13] The lines are quoted (and approved) by Bayle, *Dict.*, art. "Ovide," Remark H. The entire poem may be found in Boas, *The Happy Beast*, pp. 147 ff. See also F. Lachèvre, *Les derniers Libertins*, pp. 5-9, and 96-100.

[14] Gould's Works, II, 149 ff. Cf. Mr. Eugene H. Sloane's excellent study, *Robert Gould, Satirist*, Philadelphia, 1940.

author in every part of these travels." And the amiable
author of *The Vicar of Wakefield*—his temperament was certainly not in the least like Swift's—conforms to the same
fashion, in his verses "The Logicians Refuted. In Imitation
of Dean Swift" (1759) :

> Logicians have but ill defin'd
> As rational the human mind;
> Reason, they say, belongs to man,
> But let 'em prove it if they can. . . .
> [I] must in spite of 'em maintain,
> That man and all his ways are vain,
> And that this boasted lord of Nature
> Is both a weak and erring creature.
> That instinct is a surer guide
> Than reason—boasting mortals' pride;
> And that brute beasts are far before 'em.
> *Deus est anima brutorum.*

In all this, it is evident the satirists and other painters of
human nature in black were collaborators with the theologians, and continuers, in their own fashion, of a part of the
orthodox religious tradition; as a seventeenth-century apolo-
gist of La Rochefoucauld observed of the *Maximes* of that
author, its unflattering portrait of man's heart in its natural
state is essentially identical with that drawn by "some of
the Fathers of the Church and the great saints."[15] There is
little in La Rochefoucauld with which Pascal would have
disagreed, however much he might have added.

[15] In the *Discours* prefixed to the 1665 edition, suppressed in
the second (1666). Long attributed to Segrais, its authorship is
now regarded as uncertain.

The wide prevalence in this period of a taste for such satire, an apparent pleasure in the denigration or ridicule of man in general, may seem psychologically curious; but one may conjecture that since the thesis of man's inner corruption and perversity was so generally admitted, the average man not only became rather indurated to it and accepted it as one of the normal and proper topics for poetical and other literary exercises, but found in these at least the satisfaction of seeing vigorously and shrewdly expressed what appeared to him to be true—true, at least, of other men. Addison, however, for one, characteristically disliked the whole genre, and attacked it on the ground that it was one-sided and exaggerated and could not possibly be useful. Satires of particular types of evil or folly might be serviceable for their correction. But

> such *levelling* satires are of no use to the world, and for this reason I have often wondered how the French author [Boileau], . . . who was a man of exquisite judgment and a lover of virtue, could think human nature a proper subject for satire in one of his celebrated pieces, which is called the Satire upon Man. What vice or frailty can a discourse correct, which censures the whole species, and endeavors to show by some superficial strokes of wit, that brutes are the most excellent creatures of the two?[16]

But, as is apparent from examples already mentioned, Addison's protest did not put such satires or other general and sweeping invectives against human nature out of fashion in the ensuing half-century.

[16] *Spectator* 209; italics mine.

Vauvenargues in 1746 commented shrewdly on the motivation of this taste, and predicted that it probably would not last.

> We like to malign human nature, in order to try to raise ourselves above our species, and to gain for ourselves the respect of which we strive to rob it. We are so presumptuous that we imagine we can separate our personal interest from that of humanity in general, and malign the human race without implicating ourselves. This absurd vanity has filled the books of the philosophers with invectives against human nature. Man is at present in disgrace with all thinking men, who rival one another in charging him with depravities. But perhaps he is on the point of rising up and getting his virtues restored to him. For nothing is permanent, and there are changes of fashion in philosophy as well as in dress, music, architecture, etc.[17]

Vauvenargues' prediction was measurably true; the change of fashion had, indeed, already begun, though it was still far from abolishing the older mode in the appraisal of human nature. The denigration of man had been carried too far and been repeated too often; it is not surprising that a reaction against it and a swing in the opposite direction set in. Vauvenargues himself is one of the evidences, and one of the promoters, of this change. He is a typical transitional figure and consequently an inconsistent writer. Some of his comments on the motives from which men's actions spring are as acid as La Rochefoucauld's; but oftener he is manifestly attacking the most famous of his precursors in the same literary genre. To dwell upon *les ridicules et les faib-*

[17] *Réflexions et maximes*, p. 218.

lesses de l'humanité sans distinction does not tend to improve human nature but to deprave it;[18] "for with whatever vanity one may reproach us, we have need sometimes of being assured of our merit."[19] And on the whole, he argues, the picture which had been so often drawn of man is not and cannot be true: "If order prevails in the human race, it is proof that reason and virtue are the stronger forces in it."[20] This last argument, it may be remarked parenthetically, many theorists of human nature both before and after Vauven- argues deliberately rejected; for, as we shall see, one of their principal theses was that the good order of human society (so far as it exists) is attributable neither to reason nor to virtue. But Vauvenargues, expressing the incipient new temper, declares confidently that "real virtue, . . . which is the work of nature, and consists mainly in kindness and fortitude of soul (*la vigueur de l'ame*), will subsist forever with ineffaceable characters."[21]

4

It is, however, the older fashion in the appraisal of man that is more pertinent to the special subject of these lectures. This fashion as such, is not, I hasten to add, itself the theme of the remaining lectures; the illustrations of it already given are only by way of prelude. We shall be mainly occupied with more specific and concrete and (as I think) more construc- tive observations upon human nature than this sweeping vilification of it. Nevertheless, the general tendency of

[18] *Ibid.*, p. 285.
[19] *Ibid.*, p. 242.   [20] *Ibid.*, p. 193.   [21] *Ibid.*, p. 296.

which I have been speaking is not only an essential part of the background of the particular movement of ideas which we are to examine; it is also, as will presently appear, causally related to that movement, at least in its early phase —though the causal relation probably worked both ways.

Meanwhile, it is of some historical interest to note—still by way of prelude—that the period was perhaps, in at least one pertinent respect, more like our own than any before or since. Mr. Max Lerner, presumably having in mind the effect of certain of the new tendencies in psychology to which I have already cursorily referred, in 1939 declared that "the discovery of the irrational marks the genius of our age. . . . The intellectual revolution of the twentieth century is likely to prove the charting of the *terra incognita* of the irrational and the extraction of its implications for every area of human thought." It is, he tells us, "nothing short of a Copernican revolution in ideas," since it means that "the rational, right-thinking man has as surely ceased to be considered the center of our intellectual system as the earth has ceased to be the center of our planetary system."[22]

There is some exaggeration, I think, but also a good deal of truth in this, in so far as it relates to our own time; but "the intellectual revolution of the twentieth century"— though it *is* a revolution as against the preceding century— had its counterpart in the seventeenth and eighteenth. The writers of that age whose ideas about man's motives are to be reviewed here were also much occupied with the attempt to chart the *terra incognita* of the irrational and to extract its

[22] *The Nation*, Oct. 21, 1939.

implications. In view of their acceptance of the general
premise about human nature which we have noted, they
could hardly have failed to engage in that sort of exploration.
If man *is*, by hypothesis, in the main an irrational creature,
then, if you wish to understand man—and the age was one
in which the desire to understand him was peculiarly eager
—it is evidently for irrational (or at any rate, nonrational)
elements and forces in his nature that you must look; and, as
I have said, if you wish to control him, and to improve his
condition, it is still upon such forces that you must rely. It is
true that these older writers were usually much less systematic about it than their twentieth-century successors; they did
not, of course, anticipate all of the conclusions of the latter;
and they did not deduce complex systems of psychopathology
and psychotherapy from their premises. That they were less
penetrating is, I think, questionable; and it is not questionable that they anticipated what is, I suppose, rather widely
conceived, at least by the general educated public, to be one
of the most pregnant of contemporary discoveries in psychology. It is apparently assumed by many in our time, including Mr. Lerner, that it is a relatively recent view which
holds that men's so-called "reasons" for most of their beliefs,
as well as for their actions, are determined by their alogical
or nonrational desires; and an American expositor of Pareto
has lamented that this view still receives even from the
learned so little application in the study of human behavior.

Even the most judicious students of history and the social
sciences [Mr. L. J. Henderson has observed] hardly ever
consistently avoid the traditional assumption that the actions of men are logical. . . . Under the influence of the

desire for logical explanations, . . . which is perhaps one
of the most uniform traits of educated men, they unconsciously neglect a question that should always be considered at the outset of an inquiry: Is a certain action
logical or non-logical?[23]

The part the reaction against this assumption plays in
certain contemporary theories in sociology as well as psychology is well known. So regarded, man appears as a being
who is forever "rationalizing" but—at least in matters in
which his sentiments, passions, prejudices, or supposed interests are involved—is scarcely ever rational. He is eagerly
addicted to the use of "logic," but nearly all his logic is
upside-down; he first embraces the conclusion which is
emotionally welcome to him and then ingeniously discovers
reasons for accepting it. But, in the main, he does not do
this consciously; he believes that his ostensible reasons
really determine his conclusions or motivate his actions. He
is thus not merely nonrational but a perpetual victim of self-
deception.

But to imagine that there is anything novel in this idea is
a historical error into which no one who is even moderately
read in the theology and literature of the seventeenth and
eighteenth centuries is likely to fall. I shall cite some of the
principal evidence of the fact that the explorers of human
nature in that period were generally insistent upon the
enormous part played in human affairs by "wishful thinking"
and upon the conception of man as usually—or as some went
so far as to declare, invariably—a nonrational rationalizer.

[23] Henderson: *Pareto's General Sociology*, 1935, p. 27.

Here too it was the theological writers who seem to have started the fashion. For the doctrine of man's total depravity was a great stimulator of the quest for not only irrational but *hidden* motives behind even outwardly good acts; whatever else be said of it, it historically produced a good deal of psychological ingenuity, and a considerable amount of psychological penetration. Its defenders were bound in consistency to view with suspicion any surface show of virtue, however impressive. Men's overt behavior, it could hardly be denied, was frequently respectable, considerate, and sometimes heroic; if it were not so, if all individuals were literally and habitually "wolves," or worse, towards one another, even a moderately orderly and peaceful society could not exist. Men also professed to be actuated by reasonable or disinterested grounds of action and presumably were sometimes sincere in believing that they were. It would have been extravagant to maintain that all men are always deliberate and conscious hypocrites. To vindicate the doctrine it was necessary to penetrate below the surface of the individual's consciousness and discover the truth, of which most men were themselves unaware, about their "inward parts," about "the heart." And it was precisely the corruption of "the heart" of man, and not necessarily the invariable badness of his social conduct, that the dogma of his essential depravity usually maintained. The subtler champions of the dogma, therefore, insistently dwelt upon the thesis that, though man has undeniably been endowed by his Creator with the divine gift of reason, it is the "heart"—with a bad connotation—that controls the operations of the reason, but that in doing so the heart hides from itself, so that men are *self-*

26 *LOVEJOY*

deceivers ever. Thus "the late faithful Minister of God's Word, Daniel Dyke," wrote, before 1614, a thick volume on *The Mystery of Selfe-Deceiving; or A Discourse and Discovery of the Deceitfulnesse of Man's Heart,* published posthumously in 1630—a long preachment on the text of *Jeremiah,* 17: 9. "Peter well sayes of these corrupt lusts that they *fight against the soule*; yea, even the principall part thereof, the Understanding; by making it servilely to frame its judgement to their desire." "Our affections when they would have a thing, sharpen our wits, and set them to devise arguments to serve their turn." "Our hearts do privily and secretly (we scarce perceiving it) foist in and closely convey some corruption in our good actions."[24]

The gentle Malebranche noted that

The passions always seek to justify themselves and persuade us insensibly that we have reason for following them. The gratification and pleasure to which they give rise in the mind which should be judging them, corrupt its judgment in their favor; and thus it is that one might say that it is they which cause it to reason. . . . The passions act on the imagination, and the imagination, being corrupted, works upon the reason, always representing things to it, not as they are in themselves, . . . but as they are in relation to the present passion, so that it may pronounce the judgment that they desire.[25]

The Abbé Jacques Esprit published in 1678 an entire book

[24] *Op. cit.,* 1642 ed., p. 283; already cited by Kaye, *Mandeville's Fable of the Bees,* 1924, I, p. lxxx.

[25] *Recherche de la verité,* Bk. VI, ch. 8 and ch. 3, p. 562. See other examples from Malebranche in Kaye, *op. cit.,* I, p. lxxxi.

on this theme, *De la Fausseté des vertus humaines*,[26] which
attained considerable celebrity in its time and appeared in
an English translation in 1706.[27] Esprit especially well illus-
trates the theological motivation of this endeavor to show
that good deeds are always prompted by unworthy motives;
and it is to be borne in mind that he was not a Calvinist but a
Catholic, though of Jansenist sympathies. That the general
thesis which he proposed to elaborate in detail was already
a commonplace he admits. "Everybody owns that [men] commonly act by Interest, or Vanity." There are virtuous actions,
but these do not imply virtuous motives. "One who is Mild,
Peaceable, Indulgent, Good and Officious is not truly Virtuous, if he be so to get Men's Love, and not to obey God's
Commands." "It may always be said with Montagne: 'A virtuous action cannot be known; those that have the Good,
have not the Essence of it.' For Profit, Glory, Fear, and
such other Foreign Causes egg us on to produce them.
Valour, Justice, and Goodness may be thus called with Relation to others; but in those of whom they are asserted
they are by no means Virtues, since they have some By-End
and Motive (*il y a une autre fin proposée, une autre cause
mouvante*)." "This," says Espirit, "I design to show in this
Book"; and he accordingly seeks out the hidden causes (*les
principes cachés*) of the imperturbability of philosophers;
the probity and fidelity of men of honor, "who are so up-

[26] Paris, 1678. The book was reprinted as late as 1730.
[27] *Discourses on the Deceitfulness of humane virtues. By
Monsieur Esprit . . . Done out of French by William Beauvoir . . . To which is added, the Duke de la Rochefoucauld's reflections.* London, 1706.

right in their actions and fair in their proceedings"; the "kindness (*bonté*) of officious and charitable persons; and the magnanimity of great captains who remain undaunted in the midst of the greatest dangers."

> I wish that those in whom these Moral, Civil and Heroick Virtues shine, seeing the Vanity and Meanness of the Motives of their actions, may correct their Errors, and conceive that the Virtues they glory in are only false and sham Virtues, and that far from fancying themselves Hero's and demy Gods, they may acknowledge that they are covetous, envious, vain, weak, fickle and inconstant as other men are; . . . and that, despairing to draw any pure, solid and true virtues from so corrupt a Spring as our Nature, they may apply themselves to God to obtain them.[28]

Not even the man who goes to the scaffold rather than betray a friend can be credited with real virtue: for if you should thoroughly "probe the heart" even of so seemingly supreme an exemplar of courage and loyalty, you would find that "friendship had much less part in the action than vanity."[29]

Jean La Placette in his *Traité de l'orgueil* (1643) concisely formulated the concept of what is now called "rationalization" as follows:

> When one loves, hates, fears, desires, one has an imperative wish (*on veut absolument*) to have a reason for loving, hating, fearing, desiring . . . and by the force of one's

[28] *Deceitfulnesse of Humane Virtues*, 1706 ed.; Beauvoir's English tr., end of Preface.
[29] *De la fausseté, etc.*, p. 459.

wish for it, one imagines that one has found it—since, in truth, when one is so disposed, the weakest conjectures pass for demonstrations and the slightest surmises for certain and indubitable truths.[30]

A contemporary of Pascal had innocently remarked that his reasons (for a belief or an action) "came to him afterwards, but first the thing itself was acceptable or was offensive to him"; nevertheless, "it was offensive for the reasons which he discovered subsequently." Pascal curtly comments: "I think, not that a thing offends us for the reasons which we find afterwards, but that we find the reasons because the thing offends us."[31]

Jacques Abbadie, a French Protestant theologian famous in his day, and of considerable influence, especially in England, to which he emigrated, in his *L'Art de se connoistre soy-même* (1692) dwells at length upon "the inventiveness of the mind in discovering reasons favorable to what it desires"; for such reasons, when invented, give it pleasure, whereas "it is very slow to perceive the reasons contrary to its desire, even though they leap at the eyes, because it is irritated at finding what it was not seeking."[32] Abbadie undertakes to enumerate the principal forms of this deception of the mind by the heart: "voluntary inattention" (*les inaplications volontaires*, presumably, turning away from unwelcome evidence or the logic of an argument), "ignorances which one finds pleasurable, the errors which arise from the

[30] *Tr. de l'orgueil*, pp. 33-34.

[31] *Pensées*, ed. V. Giraud, 1924, No. 277.

[32] *Art de se connoistre soy-même*, p. 241. There were three English editions of this book.

great desire that one has of being able to deceive himself, and the *penchant* which turns our mind away from everything that is painful to it and attaches it strongly to everything that pleases it."[33]

The "light of the understanding," in short, is like physical light: "it illuminates everything, but it of itself moves nothing. It shines (*elle a du brillant*), but it has no strength. . . . If men were controlled by reason, they would be persuaded by philosophers rather than by orators. . . . *C'est que l'âme ne balance point les raisons, mais ses intérêts; et qu'elle ne pèse point la lumière, mais seulement son utilité.*"[34] This is shown by *une expérience ordinaire:* namely that "a man who has an admirable rectitude of mind and exactitude of reason for understanding what is most complex and most recondite in the sciences"—who knows when to doubt, when to affirm, when merely to opine concerning bare probabilities—"such a man is no sooner involved in some business with another, in which his own interest is involved, than his rectitude of mind deserts him, *sa raison fléchit au gre de ses désirs, et l'évidence se confond avec l'utilité.* . . . But let the same man discuss other people's affairs, and he will be found reasoning with the same correctness as before."[35] Abbadie is here expressing, and confusing, two distinct theses: first, the usual one, that it is the proper function of the reason to control action but that, in practice, it usually is itself controlled by the passions; and second, the much more radical proposition,

[33] *Ibid.*, p. 229.
[34] *Ibid.*, p. 220 f.
[35] *Ibid.*

which was to be the fundamental theorem of Hume's ethical doctrine that it is psychologically inconceivable that "reason" as such should influence volition or behavior at all. Its function is solely cognitive; it can make us acquainted with facts. But knowledge apart from desire can not determine choice:

The good attracts us; the bad repels us (*nous fait fuir*). The reason by itself does neither the one nor the other, but exists only in so far as it enables us to perceive objects [i.e., the objects open to our choice].[36]

In this persistent topic of the theologians, then, the lay satirists of man found a theme upon which endless elaboration was possible; and a great part both of La Rochefoucauld and La Bruyère consists simply in illustrations of and variations upon a single famous maxim of the former: "*l'esprit est toujours la dupe du coeur*" or, as his contemporary editor put it, "nature in man does not sincerely declare the motives which cause his actions."[37] Among Eng-

[36] *Ibid.*, p. 220.

[37] *Discours* prefixed to first edition; Flammarion ed., p. 58. Evidence of a direct transmission of the idea from the English Puritan country parson, Dyke, to the *mondain* Duke de La Rochefoucauld, has been suggested by several French scholars. For Dyke's *Mystery of Self-Deceiving* was translated into French in 1634 by a Huguenot refugee in England, Jean Verneuil, under the title *La Sonde de la Conscience*, and the French version was apparently known and admired in Jansenist circles; and the work of Esprit, a close friend of La Rochefoucauld's—he has even been called his "mentor"—was probably inspired by it. A contemporary, in an unpublished manuscript discovered in the *Bibliothèque Nationale* in the 1880's, declared that "the greater

lish secular writers, Lord Halifax tersely summed up the thesis: "Most men put their Reason out to service to their will."[38] Soame Jenyns, usually an echoer of current commonplaces of the mid-eighteenth century, did not omit this one:

Men's opinions much oftener proceed from their actions than their actions from their opinions: they act first, and then with great facility reconcile their principles to their conduct; for which reason we find . . . very few who can ever be convinced that anything is wrong from which either pleasure or profit accrues to themselves.[39]

John Adams was the principal American exponent in the later eighteenth cenury of this way of thinking, in which he was not least a child of that era—and not least an Adams. He seems to have been much impressed by the whole group of related ideas which I have been recalling. His earliest published writing, with one exception, was a little essay (1763) in which he elaborated upon the proposition that

There is nothing in the science of human nature more

part of these *Maxims* [of La Rochefoucauld] have been taken from an English book, rather badly translated into French, entitled *'La Sonde de la Conscience,'* by an English minister. . . . M. de la Rochefoucauld has merely put them into beautiful French." See E. Jovy, *Deux inspirateurs peu connus de la Rochefoucauld, Daniel Dyke et Jean Verneuil;* F. Brampton Harvey, "An English Source of La Rochefoucauld's 'Maxims,' " *The Nineteenth Century and After,* Nov., 1933, pp. 612 ff.

[38] *Works,* 1912 ed., p. 254.

[39] "Reflexions on Several Subjects," in *Works* (posthumously published, 1791), p. 342.

curious, or that deserves a critical attention from every man so much, as that principle which moral writers have distinguished by the name of self-deceit. This principle is the spurious offspring of self-love.[40]

By "self-deceit" Adams meant "rationalization" as a derivative from self-esteem—men's "disposition to flatter themselves," and consequently to "deceive themselves" to believe anything which will help them to cut a pleasing figure in their own eyes or in the eyes of others, and to present their very deficiencies in a favorable light. This "disposition" seemed to Adams to "pervade mankind from the worst to the best"—from "abandoned minds" to "those few favorites of Nature, who have received from her clearer understandings and more happy tempers than other men, who seemed designed, under Providence, to be the great conductors of art and science, war and peace, the laws and religion of this lower world."

In this propensity Adams saw "perhaps the source of far the greatest and worst part of the calamities of mankind"; but, incidentally, he characteristically pointed out—what is worth reflecting upon—the dangers, not of unconscious self-delusion, but of the consciouness of the possibility of self-delusion. A wise man is aware of the fact that his own judgments, opinions, and even moral sentiments, may, like other men's, be really formed in him, not by reason, but by "prejudices, appetites and passions which ought to hold

[40] Adams is probably here referring to a passage in Adam Smith's *Theory of Moral Sentiments*, pp. 183 f., to which I shall later refer.

a much inferior rank in the intellectual and moral system."
And, as a result, the wisest men may be the most self-dis-
trustful; "the greatest genius, united to the best disposition,
will find it hard . . . to be certain of the purity of his own
intentions." If all men were vividly and constantly aware
that the operations of their reason are but "rationalizations,"
he implies, all men would be Hamlets. But Adams' reflections on self-delusion chiefly serve to explain, for him, how
it was possible for others to hold views so different from his
own in the political controversies then beginning in Massachusetts, and why those controversies largely took the form
of "attempts to blacken and discredit the motives of the dis-
putants on both sides," rather than "rational inquiries into
the merits of the cause, the truth and rectitude of the
measures contested."[41] The reader of the essay can hardly
doubt in the end that Adams was, after all, pretty certain
that his own position on these issues was based upon such
rational considerations; and it seems evident that he
strongly resented the "blackening" of his motives for holding that position.

[41] In *The Works of John Adams,* III, pp. 433 ff., "On Self-
Delusion." Adams may be said, I think, to have been the most
assiduous American student of "social psychology" in the eighteenth century. For a later, and different, view of his on this
subject, see Lecture VII, pp. 197 ff.

Lecture II ✵ ✵ ✵

THE THEORY OF HUMAN NATURE IN THE AMERICAN CONSTITUTION AND THE METHOD OF COUNTERPOISE

We saw in the preceding lecture that in the late seventeenth and much of the eighteenth century man (as Vauvenargues put it) "was in disgrace with all thinking men" in the Western world—or at least with most of those who wrote disquisitions in prose or verse concerning him. He was described as a being actuated always by non-rational motives—by "passions," or arbitrary and unexamined prejudices, or vanity, or the quest of private economic advantage—and yet as always inwardly and incorrigibly assured that his motives *were* rational. When human nature was so conceived, it might naturally have been inferred that men were hopeless material for the construction of a peaceful, smoothly working, stable, and just political system, in which these diverse, conflicting, purely personal motivations would constantly be voluntarily subordinated to, and even made contributory to, "the general good." And such a view of human nature might well have appeared most of all incompatible with a scheme of government in which ultimate political power would be, through a wide (though still far from universal) extension of the franchise, placed in the hands of a multitude of individuals or groups prompted by such irrational and irreconcilable passions and prejudices. How could you build a safe, solid, and enduring structure out of bricks in which there were forces impelling them perpetually to push in different directions and to collide with one another? Yet it was precisely in the later eighteenth century that the scheme of "republican" government won the advocacy of political philosophers of immense influence in their time and made its first decisive advances; and (this is the particular fact relevant to our general subject which I wish to point out here) it was just at this time that the American Constitution was framed under the leadership of a group of extraordinarily able men who had few illusions about the rationality of the generality of mankind—who, in short, held in the main the theory of human nature and human motivations which was set forth in the preceding lecture.

This fact (for which I shall presently give some of the evidence) has the look of a paradox; but it is in large part (I do not say wholly) explained by the wide currency in the late seventeenth and the eighteenth century of two other conceptions, not hitherto mentioned, which implied that it is entirely possible to construct an ideal political society out of bad human materials—to frame a rational scheme of government, in which the general good will be realized, without presupposing that the individuals who exercise ultimate political power will be severally actuated in their use by rational motives, or primarily solicitous about the general good. Of these two conceptions, I shall try to elucidate and illustrate the first, which is the simpler and less far-reaching, in the present lecture; to the second we shall turn later in Lectures V and VI.

Although philosophers of the seventeenth and eighteenth centuries, when discoursing on the divine government of the world, often declared it to be axiomatic that the Creator always accomplishes his ends by the simplest and most direct means, they also tended to assume that he is frequently under the necessity of employing what may be called the method of counterpoise—accomplishing desirable results by balancing harmful things against one another. This was illustrated in the admirable contrivance on which popular expositions of the Newtonian celestial mechanics liked to dwell, whereby the planets had within them a centrifugal force which alone would have made them fly off into space in straight lines, and a centripetal force, which alone would have caused them to fall into the sun; happily counterbalancing one another, these two otherwise mischievous forces cause these bodies to behave as they should, that is, to roll round in their proper orbits. And human nature was increasingly conceived after the analogy of such a mechanical system. Voltaire proposed to amend the famous dictum of Descartes: "God, whom he called the eternal geometer, and whom I call the eternal mechanician (*machiniste*) ; and the passions are the wheels which make all these machines go."[1]

[1] *Dieu et les hommes;* cf. also *Traité de Métaphysique,* 1734, Ch. VIII. For an example of the parallel of celestial and political mechanics, *cf.* Montesquieu, *De l'Esprit des lois,* Bk. III, ch. vii: "Ambition," or the desire for "honor," which is the "principle" of the monarchical form of government, "moves all the parts of the body politic; it unites them by its own action, and the result is that each individual serves the public interest while he believes that he is serving his own. . . . You might say that it is like the system of the universe, in which there is a force which incessantly moves all bodies away from the centre and a force of gravity which brings them back to it."

The place of the method of counterpoise in the dynamics of human nature had been tersely pointed out by Pascal before 1660: "We do not sustain ourselves in a state of virtue by our own force, but by the counterpoise of two opposite faults, just as we stand upright between two contrary winds; remove one of these faults, we fall into the other."[2] La Rochefoucauld used a different simile to express the same conception: "The vices enter into the composition of the virtues as poisons enter into the composition of remedies. Prudence assembles and tempers them and makes them serve usefully against the evils of life."[3]

And the creator of a state, like the Creator of the universe and of man—and, in fact, as a *consequence* of this favorite method of the Author of Nature—must accomplish his lesser but beneficent design by pitting against one another forces (that is, human motives) which, taken separately, are disruptive or otherwise bad, or at the least nonmoral—since no other forces, no rational and virtuous motives, can be relied upon. He must harness together and counterbalance contrary defects and competing egoisms. It had been laid down by the judicious Hooker, in the earliest classic of English political thought, that

> Laws politic, ordained for external order, are never framed as they should be, unless, presuming the will of man to be inwardly obstinate, rebellious, and averse from all obedience unto the sacred laws of his nature; unless, in a word, presuming man to be in regard of his depraved

[2] *Pensées*, ed. Giraud, No. 359.
[3] *Maximes*, 182.

mind little better than a wild beast, they do accordingly
provide notwithstanding so to frame his outward actions
that they be no hindrance unto the common good for
which societies are instituted: unless they do this, they
are not perfect.[4]

This at least stated the problem: *how,* by means of what
political device, could you bring creatures whose wills were
always moved by irrational and "depraved" passions to
behave in ways which would not be inconsistent with the
"common good"? There were several proposed solutions
to the problem; the one which here concerns us and which
was to play an extremely influential part in eighteenth-
century political thinking was the method of counterpoise.
It was set forth in 1714 in doggerel verse by the very in-
judicious Mandeville. As was his custom, he put it in the
most violently paradoxical form, describing a well-ordered
state in which,

> Though every part was full of Vice,
> Yet the whole Mass a Paradise.
> Such were the Blessings of that State,
> Their Crimes conspired to make them great . . .
> The worst of all the Multitude
> Did something for the Common Good.
> This was the State's Craft that maintained
> The Whole of which each part complain'd:
> This, as in Musick Harmony,
> Made jarrings in the main agree.[5]

[4] *Laws of Ecclesiastical Polity,* I (Everyman's Library ed.,
p. 188).

[5] *The Fable of the Bees,* ed. Kaye, I, p. 24.

But the textbook—though it was a very confused textbook —on the theory of human nature which was most widely read and admired in the middle decades of the eighteenth century was provided by Alexander Pope. Every well-educated Englishman of the period, in Britain and America, was acquainted with the *Essay on Man,* and many of them doubtless knew its most famous lines by heart. And one thesis concerning the *modus operandi* of volition and the motivation of all of men's actions which the poem set forth, especially in the Second Epistle, was essentially the same as that in the lines which I have quoted from *The Fable of the Bees,* though more elegantly expressed.[6] For Pope, too, "statecraft" consisted in the recognition and application of the two premises underlying the political method of counterpoise: that men never act from disinterested and rational motives, but that it is possible, none the less, to fashion a good "whole," a happy and harmonious State, by skillfully mixing and counterbalancing these refractory and separately antagonistic parts.

Since the *Essay on Man* is, I fear, much less familiar in the twentieth than it was in the eighteenth century, it is perhaps advisable to bring together here the principal passages illustrating the summary which I have just given. Men's actions, Pope declares, are always prompted by their

[6] On the question of Pope's acquaintance with *The Fable of the Bees,* see the Introduction to A. Hamilton Thompson's edition of the *Essay on Man,* 1913, p. xi. Mr. Thompson concludes that "it is certain that Pope knew Mandeville's book," and that it "furnished a prominent portion of the argument of the Second Epistle."

passions, not by their reason. The latter, it is true, has an important part as a factor in human behavior, but it is an ancillary part. It enables us to judge of the means by which the passions, which are all "Modes of Self-Love," can be gratified, but it has no driving power.

> On life's vast ocean diversely we sail,
> Reason's the card, but Passion is the gale.[7]

The card (i.e., compass) neither propels the ship nor determines the direction in which it is to sail; it merely enables the mariner to know in which direction it is moving, or in what direction to steer in order to reach the port he desires. And the passions, which thus provide the sole dynamic factor in human behavior, are not only diverse but antagonistic to one another. Every individual's will is dominated by some obsessing "Master Passion," which is the "mind's disease":

> Reason itself but gives it edge and pow'r,
> As Heaven's blest beam turns vinegar more sour.[8]

That is one half of Pope's picture of the working of human motivations; but there is another half. Though these conflicting passions cannot be got rid of, they can be so combined and made to counteract one another that the total result will be social peace and order; and this was the purpose of the Creator in making man:

> Passions, like elements, tho' born to fight,
> Yet, mix'd and soften'd, in His work unite:

[7] Epistle II, 107-8.
[8] Epistle II, 147-8.

These, 'tis enough to temper and employ;
But what composes Man, can Man destroy? . . .
Each individual seeks a sev'ral goal,
But Heav'ns great view is one, and that the whole.
That, counterworks each folly and caprice,
That, disappoints th' effect of every vice.[9]

Thus the statesman's task is to carry out this divine purpose by so adjusting the parts of "the whole" that "jarring interests" will

of themselves create
Th' according music of the well-mixed State.

By this means it will be possible for him to

build on wants, and on defects of mind,
The joy, the peace, the glory of mankind.[10]

[9] *Ibid.*, 111 ff., 235 ff. The lines which immediately follow are pertinent rather to the ideas about human motivation which will be set forth in Lecture V. Pope fused, or perhaps confused, the two conceptions.

[10] The last two quotations are from Epistles III, 239-4 and II, 247-8. The group of passages brought together above constitute the one consistent and coherent argument, on the subject with which this lecture is concerned, that is to be found in the *Essay*. But it must be added, and emphasized, that there are other passages inconsistent with them and with one another in that highly confused poem; these are chiefly due to Pope's timidity about assigning to that traditionally venerated faculty, the Reason, the subordinate and all-but-impotent role which was essential for his principal argument and was, as shown above, frequently insisted upon by him in the most unequivocal terms. His waverings and contradictions on this matter have been well pointed out by Thompson, *op. cit.*, p. 63, n. 197.

To achieve this great end, in short, it is not at all necessary to assume that man is controlled by his reason; it is, on the contrary, necessary to assume that he is not—since that is the fact about him.

Two decades later, probably borrowing some of these ideas from Pope, the poet laureate of the time, William Whitehead, included a syncopated version of them in his poem "The Enthusiast":

> [God] bids the tyrant passions rage,
> He bids them war eternal wage,
>   And combat each his foe,
> Till from dissensions concords rise,
> And beauties from deformities,
>   And happiness from woe.

Vauvenargues wrote in 1746: "If it is true that one cannot eliminate vice, the science of those who govern consists in making it contribute to the common good." And Helvétius, later in the century, more diffusely versifies a particular form of the same general conception: every man always pursues his private interest, but the art of government lies in contriving an artificial identification of private with public interest—or at least, in persuading men that the two are identical:

> Le grand art de régner, l'Art du Législateur,
> Veut que chaque mortel qui sous ses lois s'enchaîne,
> En suivant le penchant où son plaisir l'entraîne,
> Ne puisse faire un pas qu'il ne marche à la fois
> Vers le bonheur public, le chef-d'oeuvre des lois.
> Selon qu'un Potentat est plus ou moins habile

A former, combiner cet Art si difficile,
D'unir et d'attacher, par un lien commun
A l'interêt de tous l'interêt de chacun,
Selon que bien ou mal il fonde la justice,
L'on chérit les vertus ou l'on se livre au vice.[11]

Bearing in mind these earlier statements of the two presuppositions of the method of counterpoise, as applied to the problem of government, we are now ready to turn back to what happened in Philadelphia in 1787 and, I think, to understand somewhat better what it was that then happened. To any reader of *The Federalist* it should be evident—though apparently it sometimes has not been—that the chief framers of the Constitution of the United States, who had been reared in the climate of opinion of the mid-eighteenth century, accepted the same two presuppositions and sought to apply them, for the first time in modern history, in the actual and detailed planning of a system of government not yet in existence. The ablest members of the Constitutional Convention were well aware that *their* task—unlike that of the Continental Congress of 1776—was not to lay down abstract principles of political philosophy, not to rest the system they were constructing simply upon theorems about the "natural rights" of men or of States, though they postulated such rights. Their problem was not chiefly one of political ethics but of practical psychology, a need not so much to preach to Americans about what they *ought* to do, as to predict successfully what they *would* do, supposing certain governmental mechanisms were (or were

[11] Helvétius, *Poésies*, 1781, p. 111: "Épitre sur le plaisir."

not) established. Unless these predictions were in the main correct, the Constitution would fail to accomplish the ends for which it was designed. And the predictions could be expected to prove correct only if they were based upon what—in the eyes of the chief proponents and defenders of the Constitution—seemed a sound and realistic theory of human nature.

That theory was unmistakably set forth in what has come to be the most famous of the *Federalist* papers (No. X), written by James Madison, the member of the Convention who is, I suppose, now generally admitted to deserve, if any one member can be said to deserve, the title of "Father of the Constitution."[12] Since, however, it would be unsafe to assume that the argument even of this celebrated essay is now familiar to most Americans, let me briefly summarize it, mostly in Madison's words. "The great menace," he writes, "to governments on the popular model" is "the spirit of faction." By a "faction," he explains he means "a number of citizens, whether amounting to a majority or a minority of the whole, who are united and actuated by some common impulse of passion or of interest adverse to the rights of other citizens, or to the permanent and aggregate interests of the community." There are two conceivable "methods of curing the mischiefs of faction: the one, by removing its causes, the other, by controlling its effects." The first method, however, is wholly inconsistent with popular government; you could abolish factions only by totally abolishing the "liberty" of individual citizens, i.e., their

[12] See the notable volume of Irving Brant, *James Madison, Father of the Constitution*, 1950, especially pp. 154-5.

exercise, through the franchise, of the right severally to express and to seek to realize their own opinions and wishes with respect to the policies and acts of the government. But to expect that their exercise of that right will be, in general, determined by anything but what we now call "special interests"—which is what Madison chiefly meant by "the spirit of faction"[13]—is to expect an impossible transformation of human nature. "As long as the reason of man continues fallible, and he is at liberty to exercise it, different opinions will be formed." And "as long as the connection subsists between his reason and his self-love, his opinions and his passions will have a reciprocal influence upon each other. . . . A division of society into different interests and parties" will therefore be inevitable. Since, then, "the latent causes of faction are sown in the nature of man," the "indirect and remote considerations" which are necessary to "adjust these clashing interests and render them all subservient to the public good will rarely prevail over the immediate interest which one party has in disregarding the rights of another or the good of the whole."

But though the "causes" cannot be eliminated, the "ef-

[13] The "passion" which Madison regarded as the chief source of the "spirit of faction" is economic self-interest. He was a pioneer of the conception of political struggles as, often disguised, class conflicts, and of economic determinism. But (unlike Marx) he also (to borrow Mr. Brant's summary on this point) "recognized the influence of differing opinions in religion, contrary theories of government, attachment to rival leaders, and many other points which stir the human passions and drive men into 'mutual animosities.' " (*James Madison, Father of the Constitution*, p. 173.)

fects" of the spirit of faction *can* be "controlled." How? By making sure, Madison answers, that the number and relative strength of the groups representing conflicting special interests will be such that they will effectually counterbalance one another. When they do so, no part will be able to dominate the whole, to use all the legislative and executive power of the government for its own purposes. Each faction will be unable to get a majority vote in favor of its special interest because all the other factions will be opposed to it, and thereby (Madison assumes) the "general good," or the nearest practicable approximation to it, will be realized.

In thus invoking the method of counterpoise as the solvent of the (for him) crucial problem of political theory, Madison was at the same time defending one of the chief practical contentions of the group in the Convention of which he was the leader. The question at issue, as he formulates it in *Federalist* No. X, was "whether small or extensive republics are most favorable to the public weal"; but this question did not imply that there was any conflict of opinion as to the number of states which it was desirable to include in the new Union. No one proposed the actual exclusion from membership of any of the former thirteen colonies which were willing to ratify the Constitution. The real issue concerned the apportionment of legislative authority between the national government and the States. And (at this time) Madison was an extreme advocate of "national supremacy";[14] the States should, of course, have power to make laws on strictly and obviously local concerns, but "in all cases to which the

[14] This has been conclusively shown by Mr. Brant, *cf. op. cit.*, pp. 24-25, 30-36, 60-61, and *passim*.

separate States are incompetent, or in which the harmony of the United States may be interrupted by individual legislation,"[15] that power (and adequate means to enforce its decisions) should be assigned to the Federal Congress. By an "extensive republic," then, Madison means one of this centralized sort.

As to the choice between "small" and "extensive" republics, Madison, in *Federalist* No. X, argues vigorously in favor of the latter, mainly on the ground that it alone would ensure an adequate counterbalancing of the political power of the groups representing regional (which, as he recognizes, were in America often also economic) special interests. "The smaller the society, the fewer probably will be the distinct parties and interests composing it; the fewer the distinct parties and interests, the more frequently will a majority be found of the same party, and . . . the more easily will they concert and execute their plans of oppression." But if all these clashing factions are pitted against one another in a *single* legislative body, it is unlikely that any one of them will be strong enough to carry through any such "oppressive" designs. "Extend the sphere, and you take in a greater variety of parties and interests; you make it less probable that a majority of the whole will have a common motive to invade the rights of other citizens." "Extending the sphere" meant for Madison, it is evident, increasing both the number of groups participating in the central legislative authority and

---

[15] The phrasing here is that of the "Virginia Plan." See Brant, *op. cit.*, pp. 24-25. This (as Brant has pointed out), though presented by Randolph, was merely an "echo" of Madison's proposals.

the number of subjects (touching more than merely local interests) on which it may legislate. The more "extended" it is *de jure,* the more restricted will be its power *de facto.* The decisive "advantage," in short "of a large over a small republic" will "consist in the greater obstacles opposed to the concert and accomplishment of the secret wishes of an unjust and interested majority."

All this should be sufficient to justify the conclusion which I earlier propounded in advance of the proof of it, i.e., that the fundamental political philosophy of Madison (at this time) included two crucial propositions: (1) that the political opinions and activities of individuals will, with perhaps the rarest exceptions, always be determined by personal motives at variance with the general or "public" interest—in short, by bad motives; but (2) that, in framing a political constitution, you can construct a good whole out of bad parts, can make these conflicting private interests subservient to the public interest, simply by bringing all of them together upon a common political battleground where they will neutralize one another.

It has seemed to me worth while to present evidence for the first point at considerable length because there appears to be a still widely prevalent belief among Americans that the Founding Fathers were animated by a "faith in the people," a confidence in the wisdom of "the common man." This belief, to use the terminology of the logic books, is a grandiose example of the fallacy of division. For Madison, as we have seen—and in this he probably did not differ from the majority of his colleagues in the Convention—had *no* "faith in the people" *as individuals* acting in their political capacity. It is true that he recognized certain political *rights* of individual citizens—primarily the right to vote (with the large exceptions, *inter alia*, of women and Negroes) and to seek public office. It is also true that he sincerely believed, as apparently did many of his colleagues, that they themselves were distinterestedly constructing a scheme of government which would make for the good of the people as a whole and in the long run.[16] But "the people" as voters, the total electorate, was made up wholly of "factions," i.e., of individuals combined into rival political groups or parties; and a faction always strives to accomplish ends "adverse to the rights of other citizens, or to the permanent and aggregate interests of the community." "Faith in the people" is plainly and vigorously repudiated in *Federalist* No. X. But what Madison did have faith in was the efficacy, and probable adequacy, of the method of counterpoise as a corrective of the evils otherwise inevitably resulting from "government on the popular model," a "republican remedy for the diseases most incident to republican government."

One fundamental thesis in this lecture, the learned reader will note, precisely contradicts a historical generalization set

[16] This assumption of the disinterestedness of the makers of a Constitution—their exemption from the motivations controlling the political behavior of the rest of mankind—was psychologically almost indispensable in the Convention; certainly, few were likely to admit frankly that their own arguments were simply expressions of the "spirit of faction." But that they usually were so in fact is, I take it, now recognized by all competent historians; there are, indeed, few better examples of Madison's thesis—the shaping of political opinions by private, class, or sectional interests—than are to be found in the debates of the Convention.

forth in a celebrated, learned and brilliantly written book by
a recent American historian. Carl Becker's *The Heavenly
City of the Eighteenth-Century Philosophers* offers an enum-
eration of "four essential articles of the religion of the
Enlightenment"; two of these articles are: "(1) Man is
not natively depraved; . . . (3) Man is capable, guided solely
by the light of reason and experience, of perfecting the good
life on earth. . . . The Philosophers . . . knew instinctively
that 'man in general' is natively good, easily enlightened,
disposed to follow reason and common sense, generous and
humane and tolerant, easily led by persuasion more than
compelled by force; above all, a good citizen and a man of
of virtue." That there were some writers in the eighteenth century who would have subscribed to these articles,
and that a tendency to affirm them was increasing, especially
in France in the later decades of the century, is true. That
the conception of the character and dominant motives of
"man in general" formulated by Becker in the sentences
quoted was held by most, or even by the most typical and
influential, "eighteenth-century philosophers" is not true;
it is a radical historical error. To assume its truth is to fail
to see the most striking feature of the most widely prevalent
opinion about human nature current in the period and to
misapprehend the nature of the peculiar problem with which
the "enlightened" and innovating political and social theorists and statesmen of that age were dealing. The question
here, of course, like all historical questions, is one to be
settled chiefly by documentary evidence; and it is partly for
that reason that I have cited the *ipsissima verba* of the de-
signers of our own Constitution. To these let us now return.

It is not solely in his argument on the division of powers between the national and state government, in the tenth *Federalist* paper, that Madison rests his case upon the two propositions of which I have been speaking. In his defense of all the major provisions of the Constitution concerning the internal structure of the national government itself—its division into three departments (legislative, executive, and judicial), the division of the legislature into two houses, the whole scheme of "checks and balances"—the same two premises are fundamental and decisive. When Madison undertakes to justify the separation of the Federal government into three mutually independent departments, his distrust of human nature and his conception of the way to offset its defects in planning a system of government are even more sharply expressed than in No. X. I hope those who are familiar with the text of *The Federalist* will forgive me for quoting from it at some length, for the benefit of those to whom it is not familiar:

The great security against a gradual concentration of the several powers in the same department, consists in giving to those who administer each department *the necessary means, and personal motives, to resist the encroachments of the others.* The provision for defence must in this case, as in all others, be made commensurate to the danger of attack. *Ambition must be made to counteract ambition. The interests of the man must be connected with the constitutional rights of the place.* It may be a reflection on human nature, that such devices should be necessary to control the abuses of government. *But what is government itself but the greatest of all reflections on human nature?*

. . . The policy of supplying, by opposite and rival inter-
ests, the defects of better motives might be traced through
the whole system of human affairs, private as well as public. We see it particularly displayed in all the subordinate
distribution of power; where the constant aim is . . . that
the private interest of every individual may be sentinel
over the public interest.[17]

And this policy, Madison declares, is completely exemplified
in the Constitution, which was then awaiting ratification.

In the Federal Republic of the United States, whilst all
authority in it will be derived from, and dependent on the
society, the society itself will be broken into so many
parts, interests, and classes of citizens, that the rights of
individuals, or of the minority, will be in little danger
from interested combinations of the majority. In a free
government, the security for civil rights must be the same
as that for religious rights. It consists in the one case in
the multiplicity of interests, and in the other in the multiplicity of sects. The degree of security in both cases will
depend on the number of interests and sects; and this

[17] *The Federalist*, No. LI; italics mine. Long attributed to
Hamilton, this paper is now known to have been written by
Madison; *cf.* Brant, *op. cit.*, pp. 184 and 486, n. 12. It should be
mentioned that in a single sentence in this essay Madison
writes: "A dependence on the people is, no doubt, the primary
control on the government; but experience has taught mankind
the necessity of auxiliary precautions." But this seems no more
than a prudent recognition of the fact that the general mass of
voters possesses ultimate political power; and what Madison
thought of "the people," in this sense, we have already seen. His
chief concern was to prove the indispensability of the "auxiliary
precautions." For the full presentation of the evidence that No.

may be presumed to depend on the extent of country and the number of people comprehended under the same government.[18]

In short, the bigger the country ("provided it lies within a practicable sphere"), the greater the assurance that "a coalition of the majority of the whole society could seldom take place upon any other principles than those of justice and the general good." It must be remembered that, in Madison's opinion, no coalition based upon *these* principles is likely except, perhaps, in times of grave national danger. Under such circumstances, there may be virtually universal agreement as to the measures necessary to avert the danger. But under normal conditions, the people will always be divided into factions, and it is essential that no faction—in other words, no *fraction* of the people—shall ever obtain a majority in the legislature. This, however, can easily be prevented by means of the counterposition of the factions to one another.

Madison's thesis here, then, may be summed up thus: The whole people has the sole right to rule, but no mere majority, *however large,* has that right. This seems a political paradox; but as actually applied—primarily, in the situation confronting the Convention itself—it resulted in the adoption of a series of compromises with which no faction

---

I, II, and the two preceding and seven following *Federalist* papers were composed by Madison, see Edward G. Bourne's study, "The Authorship of the *Federalist,*" in his *Essays in Historical Criticism,* 1901.

[18] *Ibid.*

was wholly satisfied, but which all, after much wrangling, were willing to accept, *faute de mieux*. Being under the practical necessity of arriving at *some* agreement, they reached a reluctant unanimity (barring a few irreconcilable individuals) made necessary by the approximate counter-balancing of the conflicting groups and interests represented. And when embodied in the Constitution, these compromises for a time—though with steadily increasing tensions—*worked;* they held the Union together for more than seventy years. In this sense, and to this extent, Madison's theoretical principles may be said to have been pragmatically vindicated.

Lest it be supposed that faith in the method of counterpoise was peculiar to Madison among the members of the Convention, let me cite one more example from a member very different in temperament and character and in many of his opinions on specific issues. In the discussion of the powers of the "second branch" of the Federal legislature—i.e., the Senate—Gouverneur Morris delivered a characteristic speech in which he declared that the essential function of such a second chamber is "to check the precipitation, changeableness and excesses of the first branch." But "what qualities are necessary to constitute a check in this case? . . . The checking branch must have a personal interest in checking the other branch. One interest must be opposed to another interest. Vices as they exist must be turned against each other." Morris regarded the Senate—whose members, he thought, should hold office for life—as representing the interest of the propertied class. Doubtless, "the rich will strive to establish their dominion and to enslave the rest. They always did; they always will. The proper security against them is to form them into a separate interest. The two forces will then control each other. By thus combining and setting apart the aristocratic interest, the popular interest will be combined against it. There will be a mutual check and a mutual security." As the body representative of those who have "great personal property," the Senate will "love to lord it through pride. Pride is indeed, the great principle that actuates the poor and the rich. It is this principle which in the former resists, in the latter abuses, authority."[19]

But though Morris here voiced the same opinion of human motives that we have seen expressed by Madison and also, in order to offset the absence of "better motives," relied upon the counterbalancing of bad ones, he was in fact employing partially identical premises to support a different conclusion. For Madison, when writing in *The Federalist*, assumed that there would always be a "multiplicity" of such special interests and that the numerical ratios of the groups severally supporting them, or of their representatives in Congress, would be such that no coalition of them could ever obtain a majority.[20] But Morris—at least when

[19] Elliot's *Debates on the Adoption of the Federal Constitution,* V (1870), pp. 270 f.

[20] Why Madison made this assumption may seem at first hard to understand; he writes as if he, like Pope, accepted as evident beyond the need of proof the assumption that "jarring interests" will *"of themselves* create th' according music of the well-mix'd State"—though Madison adds, in substance, that they will not be well-mixed unless the mixture comprises *all* of them, in an "extensive republic." As a generalization the assumption was

making this speech—recognized only two permanently opposed forces in politics, the rich and the poor. And he cannot, of course, have supposed that these two would usually, or, indeed, ever, numerically counterbalance one another. They must therefore be *made* equal in legislative power—or, more precisely, in legislative impotence—by a specific constitutional provision; one of the Houses of Congress must be reserved for men having great wealth and the "aristocratic spirit," an American analogue of the House of Lords. True, Morris grants—human nature being what it is—such a body will always be inimical to the interests of "the rest," the nonpropertied classes. It is therefore necessary to have another chamber representative of the latter, to hold in check the former. But it is not in this latter consideration that Morris seems chiefly interested. What he wished to ensure was the protection of the vested interests of large property-holders. And he saw that the method of counterpoise, especially in the form which he proposed, was

---

certainly not self-evident, nor particularly probable. But in fact Madison had specific reasons for the assumption, which he set forth in his speech in the Convention on June 28, 1787. He was then arguing (unsuccessfully, as it turned out) in favor of giving to the larger states more Senators than to the small states. To the objection that this would enable the larger states to combine to dominate the smaller ones, he replied that this could happen only if the larger states had common "interests," which they did not have. The three largest were Massachusetts, Pennsylvania, and Virginia. These were remote from one another; they differed in "customs, manners, and religion"; and, still more important, their trade interests were entirely "diverse." "Where," then, "is the probability of a combination? What the inducements?" Thus, it will be seen, Madison was here asserting an *actual*

perfectly adapted to the accomplishment of this end. For
the effect of that method, when applied to a legislative body,
would be—as Madison's arguments said—to prevent any
one of the opposing factions from ever accomplishing its
purpose. A Senate that was representative exclusively of one
economic class would never concur in any measure affecting class interests passed by a House that was representative of other classes. And it followed that "the poor" could
never get a law passed which would be unfavorable to the
economic interests of "the rich."[21]

Thus the method of counterpoise could, without relin-
quishment of its two essential premises, be proposed as a
means to the realization of quite different designs with
respect to the distribution of legislative power. But, whatever the purpose for which it might be advocated, it obviously could have only negative effects. It was simply a way
of *preventing* new proposals from being adopted. If it ever
became completely effective (which, of course, it never

existing counterpoise of political forces in the Federal Union:
where there is no identity of economic and other interests, there
can be no "coalition," and therefore no majority in Congress for
any one group. But since the proposal of unequal state representation in the Senate failed to carry, he turned, in the *Federalist*, to another and less specific argument: be the states equally
or unequally represented in the "second chamber," there would
in any case be a natural counterbalancing of voting strength
among such a "multiplicity" of sections and economic interests
and religious sects. And though Madison now gave no definite
or cogent reasons for believing this to be true, it *was* true, subject to the qualifications above noted.

[21] Madison, in spite of his usual argument based upon the
existing multiplicity of interests and factions, recognized, like

quite did), it could result only in a deadlock, an equi-
librium of forces in which no movement in any direction
would be possible. It therefore tended to crystallize the
status quo and was naturally favored by those who wished
to keep the existing political and economic order unchanged
—or as little changed as possible. It was a device of conser-
vatives to block innovations. Yet it could hardly be openly
argued for upon traditionally conservative grounds—e.g.,
upon the assumption that change is in itself a bad thing or
that the "aristocratic" and propertied class is wiser than,
and morally superior to, the "lower classes." For it rested,
as we have seen, upon the generalization that (certainly in
politics) the aims and motives of virtually all individuals,
and therefore of all "factions," are equally irrational and
"interested," equally indifferent to the "general good";
and it was *only* upon this assumption that the scheme of
equipoise, of rendering all factions *equally* impotent, could
be consistently defended.

But this generalization, though indispensable to the argument, had some awkward consequences. It implied that, in
political discussion and agitation, appeals to purely ethical

Morris, that the most serious conflict within the Union was that
between only two factions; but for him, this was not a conflict
between "the rich" and "the poor," but between two major sections of the country. In a memorably prophetic speech on June
29th he warned the Convention that "the great danger to our
general government is, the great southern and nothern interests
being opposed to each other. Look to the votes in Congress [i.e.,
of the Confederation], and most of them stand divided by the
geography of the country, not according to the size of the
States." This supreme danger he hoped and believed could be

standards and rational and disinterested ideals would be
inappropriate and useless, since, by hypothesis, no such appeal could really influence the opinions and actions of the
voters or legislators. But in practice such moral, or ostensi-
bly moral, appeals were *not entirely* ineffective; and, once
organized political parties were actually operating, their
orators seldom, if ever, admitted that the policies they
advocated were adverse "to the rights of others and the
good of the whole"; on the contrary, they usually represented these policies as consistent with, or even required by,
the highest moral principles, and they doubtless often believed this to be true. And though this usually was—and
still is—simply "rationalization," even a rationalization is
an admission that rational considerations, valid by criteria
which are more than biases arising from private interests
or from unexamined and unverifiable preconceptions, are
relevant to the issue under discussion. However small the
part which such considerations really play in the determination of individual opinions and individual behavior, as
soon as you admit their relevance, and profess to justify
your own contentions by them, you have accepted a change
of venue to another and admittedly a higher court, in
which the controversy must be fought out under the rules of
that court, that is, rules of logical consistency and verifiable

averted by means of a balance of power in Congress between
the two sections. So long as, by various compromises, that balance seemed to remain approximately undisturbed, Madison's
hope was realized. As soon as the balance was patently over-
thrown, the danger which he pointed out became a tragic
reality.

empirical evidence. In so far as those who invoked the method of counterpoise implicitly denied even the possibility of such a change of venue, they ignored a real aspect of the workings of human nature in politics. But in saying this I am far from intending to imply that their assumptions about men's usual motivations, in their political opinions and actions, were false, or even that they were not the *more* pertinent and useful assumptions to apply to the immediate practical problems which confronted the Constitution-makers in 1787.

In these comments on the latent implications, the degree of validity, and the practical effect of the theory of counterpoise which so powerfully influenced the framing of the American Constitution, I have deviated from the primarily historical purpose of the present lecture. That purpose was not to evaluate but to illustrate the wide prevalence, even in the later eighteenth century, of a highly unfavorable appraisal of the motives generally controlling men's political (and other) behavior, and to explain in part the seemingly paradoxical fact that, in the very same period, the American republic was founded, largely by men who accepted that appraisal. This purpose has, I hope, now been sufficiently accomplished.

But there was, as I have already said, another idea, or complex of interrelated ideas, about the springs of action in men, which throughout the seventeenth and eighteenth centuries was even more widely prevalent than the conceptions underlying the method of counterpoise; and it had a broader scope, and could lead in part to different conclusions. Both, it is true, were in agreement on one funda-

mental premise already familiar to us: the assumption that
man's "reason" has, at most, a secondary and a very small
influence upon his conduct and that irrational or nonrational feelings and desires are the real efficient causes of
all, or nearly all, of men's actions. And there followed
from this assumption the practical corollary that one who
wishes to control men's "outward conduct"—i.e., by means
of a system of government—must do so by *employing* these
nonrational forces, must (as Pope had said) "build on
wants, and on defects of mind" the social and political
structure which he seeks to realize.

Inasmuch as this general assumption underlay both the
theory already expounded—that embodying the principle of
counterpoise—and what as yet I can only refer to (since it
has not yet been expounded) as the second theory, they may
be considered species of the same genus. And, having thus
one fundamental presupposition in common, they have
often been lumped together as identical—by Pope, among
others. But they were actually, in other respects, extremely
dissimilar. Whereas the scheme of counterpoise, in order
to offset the irrational and mutually antagonistic motivations of individuals, relied upon an essentially external,
political, and quasi-mechanical device, the second theory
found in the individual—in all individuals—a certain
peculiarly potent type of motivation which, though admittedly a mode of self-love and certainly not "rational," was
not necessarily mutually antagonistic or "adverse to the
common good," but, on the contrary (as many writers
maintained, though others denied), consisted of subjective
forces which give rise to socially desirable "outward con-

duct," apart from any external controls. Since I have not yet explained what the second theory is or given historical examples of it, this indication of the specific difference (within a generic identity) between it and the theory previously outlined will probably sound rather obscure; nevertheless, the general nature of that difference should, I think, be made explicit at this point, before we go on to the exposition and illustration of the second theory. That theory offers (I think) a more penetrating insight into human nature than any which we have thus far considered. But the seventeenth and eighteenth-century expressions of it were involved in some serious terminological confusions, and they also often failed to bring out its most significant implications. In order that we may understand these confusions and these implications better, I shall, in the next lecture, jump over those centuries and, abandoning temporarily the role of historian, attempt some reflections on certain features of human nature from the point of view— or *a* point of view—of our own time.

Lecture III

THE DESIRES OF THE
SELF-CONSCIOUS ANIMAL

The student of the history of ideas must approach his historical sources certainly with an open but not with a passive mind. The profitable reading of a text which contains any but the simplest ideas is always a process of cross-examination—of putting relevant questions to the author; and the reader must therefore know in advance what questions need to be asked. To ask the right questions, the reader must first of all consider what distinctions—between concepts and therefore between terms—are pertinent and important in relation to the topics or issues with which the author is concerned. Many—most, I am inclined to think—of the terms which have historically been used in the expression of more or less abstract ideas have been ambiguous terms, and a great many of the propositions which have played influential parts in the history of thought have been equivocal propositions. For this reason, if you wish to know what an author means by his terms or propositions, it is desirable to have in mind in advance, as far as possible, what different things he *might* conceivably mean by the words he uses. You may then sometimes, by analysis and comparison of different passages, discover which of these distinguishable things he does mean; but if the precaution of making such distinctions beforehand is neglected, there is always a risk that you will impose a wrong, or an oversimple, meaning on his words from the outset, and thus more or less completely misinterpret him.

Moreover, it frequently happens that an author, without being aware of it himself, uses the same words in different senses—slips insensibly from one meaning to another in the course of an exposition or argument. There is perhaps no more frequent source of error in interpretation than to assume that a given author always uses the same crucial term in the same sense—even though he may have himself offered, at the outset, a definition of the term. Such unconscious shifts of meaning can, of course, be detected only by a close scrutiny of the contexts—and especially of the inferences which the author draws from verbally identical or similar propositions at different points in his reasoning. If, in one place, he deduces from a proposition a consequence which patently would not follow if he were using the words in it in the same sense in which he has used them in another place, it is probable that, though the words are the same, the ideas present (less or more vaguely) to his consciousness in the two places are different ideas.

And, at least for the intellectual historian, the object of reading is, if possible, not simply to note what an author literally *says* in a given passage, but what, and how, he was thinking when he said it—what concepts were, dimly or otherwise, in his mind and by what processes of thought he actually passed from one proposition to another. This is often a difficult and delicate business. But one does not, in most cases, adequately understand an author—does not see what was going on in him as he wrote—unless one understands him better than he understood himself. And for this purpose, again, it is highly desirable to bring to the reading of a writer's text, not only some previous reflection on the subject with which he is dealing, but, especially, as many distinctions of meaning potentially pertinent to it, and of issues involved in it, as possible. With the help of these, you may frequently discover which of your author's terms are equivocal and therefore of indeterminate meaning; or into what inexplicit, and therefore presumably unconscious, shifts of meaning he slips; and to what confusions of ideas he is subject; and what are the resultant illicit (though to him convincing) transitions in his reasoning.

The principal purpose of this preamble to the present lecture is to explain why it has seemed to me desirable to interpolate at this point what might otherwise appear to be an incomprehensible digression from the mainly historical subject of the course. The subsequent lectures will have to do chiefly with ideas widely current in the seventeenth and eighteenth centuries about a certain group of human motives or desires, about their social consequences, and about their implications for the appraisal of human nature. The terminology the writers of the period used, however, was often confused and inconsistent. We shall therefore be better prepared to understand what those writers had to say about these matters if we make explicit to ourselves in advance a few simple distinctions, adopt convenient terms for expressing them, give a little thought beforehand and from our present point of view—or at any rate, from the lecturer's —to the nature and interrelations of those elements of our constitution with which these older analysts of it were especially preoccupied, and consider what there is about them that makes them seem significant for the general theory of man. The present lecture, then, is an attempt to construct for ourselves some fragments of what in the seventeenth century would probably have been called a *Traité des Passions*.

1

It is not, however, with "passions" in the etymological sense, which the word sometimes retained in seventeenth and eighteenth century use—i.e., in the sense of passive states of sensation or emotion—that we shall be concerned in this lecture. It is with the question what affective states operate as the distinctive *springs of action* in man and how they so operate. We are more specifically to consider, first of all, the nature of what are commonly called desires and motives, and the ways in which they appear to determine more or less deliberate voluntary choices, decisions by human agents to act in one or another manner, when the thought of the act to be performed and of its alternative is—though it may be but dimly and momentarily—present to consciousness before the act takes place. We may begin by defining some pertinent terms. Implicit in these definitions are some postulates or factual assumptions, which, though familiar, are not universally accepted; but it will be more convenient to state the definitions and postulates first, and then consider the objections to them.

The primary phenomenon pertinent to deliberate voluntary action may be called "hedonic susceptibility in the experiencing subject to the idea of a state-of-things." A state-of-things may be anything whatever that can be conceived as capable of existing or occurring in the past, present, or future; thus an act of your own not yet performed would be included under the denotation of "state-of-things." To the *ideas* of states-of-things pleasant or unpleasasnt feelings may be, and usually are, attached; that is to say, the presence of such ideas in consciousness is agreeable, satisfying, welcome, or the reverse. A *specific* hedonic susceptibility is the capacity of a subject or class of subjects to find pleasant or unpleasant the presence in consciousness of a particular idea or sensation. A *desire* occurs when the idea of a state-of-things not now realized, or, if now realized, capable of prolongation into the future, is present to consciousness, and the idea of its realization (or prolongation) is *now* found pleasant, and of its nonrealization or cessation, painful. *Aversion* is the opposite of this: when the idea of the realization of a state-of-things is now unpleasant. Desires and aversions may differ very widely in intensity, i.e., in the intensity of the pleasantness or unpleasantness attaching to the ideas. At least the more intense desires or aversions tend to be followed by *actions* conceived by the subject as capable of causing, or helping to cause, the realization of the state-of-things of which the idea of the realization is pleasant, or preventing the realization of that of which the idea of its realization is unpleasant—unless there is at the same time present to consciousness a contrary and still more intense desire or aversion. A *motive* is a specific desire or aversion, i.e., a pleasant or unpleasant idea of a realizable state-of-things, when it functions as the actual determinant of an

action. What at least ordinarily and normally determines
choice, among alternative possible courses of action, is the
relative intensity of the pleasantness or unpleasantness
attaching, *at the moment preceding choice*, to the *ideas* of
the two or more possible courses of action—*not necessarily
the anticipated pleasantness or unpleasantness of their future
results*. This pleasantness, or its opposite, may *either attach
to the idea of the action in itself*, or may be derivative from
the idea of the anticipated pleasantness or unpleasantness
of the consequences of the action.

The first objection which some psychologists would raise
to the foregoing definitions is that they seem to presuppose
that mental states or mental "contents"—ideas, or the feelings associated with them—cause or determine bodily behavior, which, according to a metaphysical dogma accepted
by these psychologists, is quite impossible. This objection,
however, we need not here attempt to refute. It is not
necessary, for our present purpose, to become involved in
the old controversy over the so-called mind-body problem.
With those who hold that the actual determinants of those
movements of organic matter which we call human behavior
are those other antecedent states or movements of matter
and energy, or energy alone, which consist in patterns or
motions of particles or energy-quanta in the brain and
nervous system—with those who hold this view I shall not
now quarrel. I think their view untenable, but the assumption of its untenability is not essential to our present analysis. It may be true not only that every nuance of feeling,
every desire and every purpose, has its specific neurocerebral
antecedent, but also that these physical events alone are

efficacious, while consciousness and all its content are a sort of *obbligato*—in Santayana's phrase, merely "a lyric cry in the midst of business." Even if this be true, it means only that two types of event, one conscious, the other unconscious, are uniformly associated. And of the two sides or "aspects" of the total event, the neurocerebral side is, for the most part, at the time of the occurrence of the event, quite inaccessible and unknown to us, and is also incapable of being directly acted upon. I know what it is to be angry, or happy, or proud; I do not know what particular neural or cortical patterns accompany anger or happiness or pride. I also know that I can be made angry or happy or proud by words addressed to me, if—but only if—I regard those words as expressing ideas, i.e., as having for those who use them certain meanings, and not as mere sounds, that is, motions in the atmosphere which impinge on my ear-drums and thence start further movements or energy-discharges in the auditory nerve which presently reach a certain region in my brain, and there cause a certain unknown rearrangement of the bits of matter or units of energy composing it. Some of these motions certainly are, all of them may be, indispensable to the production of the effect called feeling angry or feeling happy or feeling proud. But I never experience the immediate intracerebral counterpart of the anger, happiness, or pride; I do experience the fact that when I feel angry or happy or proud I am likely to speak and act in a specific manner. And I assume all this to be true of other organisms of my own species. We shall, therefore, limit our analysis to what we empirically know and, in some degree, know how to control—that is, to actually experienced feelings, desires, thought-content, purposes—and their observable consequences or sequels in the form of other conscious events or in physical behavior (including speech); and we shall leave special questions of brain-physiology and of the correlation of cortical with conscious states to the as yet rather difficult and tentative inquiries of the brain-physiologists.

Now the word "desire" seems to be somewhat going out of fashion among psychologists—partly, I venture to think, for good and partly for bad reasons—and is being replaced by such terms as "drive," "urge," "organic impulsion," or "bodily set." One of the good reasons is that recent psychologists have realized more clearly than some earlier ones that, if we are to find anything that can be called a causal explanation of the eventual adoption of one course of action rather than another, in the situation we are considering, it must consist in some element or factor—whether explicit in consciousness or not—that is prior to or simultaneous with the initiation of that course of action, something which may be—though this, like the word "drive," is pure metaphor—described as a push rather than a pull. But the term "desire," as ordinarily used, tends to suggest a pull. A desire presumably is directed upon a future object, and to speak of desires as determining action may suggest that it is some character of the future object that *zieht uns hinan*—an Aristotelian final cause. But, though final causes certainly have much to do with human action, they can be seriously supposed to determine it only when they are translated into the present tense—are connected with some already existing state or propension in the organism before it acts. And the primary

problem of the analysis of the phenomena commonly named
desire and choice is to ascertain, if possible, of what sorts
these antecedent states or propensions are. Another reason
for the new fashion in terminology which is valid, up to a
point, is a recognition of the fact that there are various
specific chains or cycles of actions which, once started,
tend, in animals in general, to run their course; one stage
leads on automatically to the next, and the following of one
upon the other is to be understood, at least in part, by a
knowledge of the character of the total sequence and of the
empirical law which describes its usual successive phases.
This appears to be what is meant by a "drive." Even the
word "motive" is translated by Woodworth into the expression "an activity in process"; the motive, if I may employ
the term, of this translation is apparently a wish to simplify
the whole problem by conceiving of all cases of choice
after the analogy of a fixed row of blocks—the fall of the
first block pushes the next one down, and so on; no conscious reference to the future is necessarily involved in the
affair.

Now there are, no doubt, modes of determination of
human as of animal behavior which have this simple, auto-
matic character; but they are assuredly not the only modes,
nor, in man, the most distinctive. We do experience desires,
in the sense previously defined—that is, we consciously
refer to future states-of-things, whether in our own experience or not, and we find pleasurable the *idea* of their realization or painful the idea of their nonrealization; when one
such idea is present and central in the field of consciousness, we normally tend to the course of action which we

conceive as likely to realize that future-but-now-represented state-of-things. This appears to me the merest commonplace; but since it is sometimes questioned or disregarded, I can only ask you to judge for yourself—to recall and analyze your own experience or, for example, the occasion when, after viewing those seductive pictures, in an illustrated weekly, of other human creatures riding in luxurious motor-cars, you found the desire to possess one of these vehicles irresistible. Equally open to every man's retrospective introspection, presumably, is the case in which two such representations of future states-of-things were, before an action is initiated, compresent in consciousness, both pleasurable and therefore both evoking desire—until, somehow, the action believed to make for the realization of one rather than the other got chosen.

Ordinarily and normally, then, it is here assumed, pleasurableness and unpleasurableness of the ideas of realizable states do determine choice; but this is not to say that they are the invariable determinants. There are, it may be urged, exceptional cases in which the unpleasant has an irresistible allurement—probing an aching tooth, for example, or obsessing moods of self-reproach or self-dissatisfaction. The *universal* connection of pleasantness or unpleasantness with desire or aversion need not be asserted, but only their usual connection. But it is important at this point to bear in mind a simple distinction, which is now, I suppose, fairly well realized, though the neglect of it has in the past caused much confusion and error, especially in the history of ethical theory.

Supposing pleasantness or unpleasantness to be normally

elements in the complex states called desires and aversions and to be factors in the determination of choice, *to what* do they attach—what, in particular, is the relative *time* to be assigned to them? According to what may be called the classic conception of desire and choice—a conception which, from the time of Socrates, was dominant in ethical theory, and is still current—what takes place in consciousness at the moment preceding choice is the presentation for awareness of the idea of an end or ends which might be realized through one's action, and a forecast of the *future* enjoyableness of one or another end. When the choice is made, it is supposed to be always determined by the anticipated *eventual* satisfyingness—the satisfyingness for the chooser or for somebody—of the end *when it shall be reached,* be the end a good dinner tomorrow, or the classless society, or the joys of the Moslem paradise, or the beatific vision of the divine perfection. All choice, in short, according to the thesis repeated in varying terms by a thousand moral philosophers, is *sub specie boni;* and these philosophers have therefore disputed chiefly *de finibus bonorum et malorum*—about the generic nature of the "real" or "highest" good, that is, the kind of state-of-things which will most completely and lastingly satisfy such a being as man is. Jonathan Edwards summed it up with precision:

> The greatest good proposed [i.e., anticipated] and the greatest evil threatened, when equally believed and reflected on, is sufficient to engage the Will to choose the good and refuse the evil, and is that alone which doth move the Will to choose or to refuse. . . . [Hence], the determinations of the Will must evermore follow the

illumination, conviction and notice of the Understanding, with regard to the greatest good and evil proposed, reckoning both the degree of good and evil understood, and the degree of understanding, notice and conviction of that proposed good and evil; and . . . it is thus necessarily, and can be otherwise in no instance; because it implies a contradiction, to suppose it ever to be otherwise.[1]

Similarly, the psychological hedonism of the Utilitarians of the nineteenth century usually assumed that choice is controlled by the preconceived *future* pleasurableness of the end, or desired state-of-things: in John Stuart Mill's famous thesis,[2] "desiring a thing and finding *it* pleasant are but different names for the same fact." Even some recent and elaborate analyses of volition seem not wholly exempt from this assumption of the determination of choice by the foreseen (or imagined) satisfyingness of the consummation of the present desire or interest.

But this is, I believe, a simple psychological error—an error about the time at which pleasantness and unpleasantness is or are operative as determinants of voluntary choice.[3] The future as such, as we have already remarked, is not the efficient cause of the present, and an "end," a "good proposed," or final cause, must somehow be repre-

[1] *Freedom of the Will*, p. 9, in *Works*, N. Y. 1881, p. 49.

[2] The passage here cited does not set forth the whole of Mill's ethical doctrines by any means; but it appears to express the psychological premise which he regarded as substantiating that doctrine.

[3] There is, it is true, a form of hedonism which does not fall into this error. It is what Troland has named the "hedonism of the present."

sented by a present surrogate if it is to be supposed to influence present choice or action. The affective determinant of deliberate desire is, then, the felt relative pleasantness or welcomeness of an *idea* of a future state-of-things *at the moment of choice*—the *present valuedness of the idea*, not the anticipated future value of the state-of-things.[4]

Now at such a moment there are two quite distinct kinds of ideas of future states-of-things which may be present for awareness (future in the sense of subsequent to *that* moment), namely, the idea of the end, or the state-of-things conceived as potentially *resulting from* the choice and the act, and the idea of *the choice or the act itself, or of oneself conceived as choosing or acting in a certain manner.* And (this is a crucial proposition in the present argument, the presupposition of a certain conclusion of which the importance will appear more fully later), the chooser's idea of himself as possessing and manifesting *in* his contemplated act certain qualities or powers or characteristics which he can *now* at the moment of choice regard with pleasure (or at least without displeasure) can, and often does, have present value, i.e., is a determinant of desire. This desire has no necessary or fixed connection with the desire for ends, or termini of action, conceived as about-to-be-satisfying when attained. The wish to *get* or achieve something *by* one's act, and the wish to *be* something *in* one's act, are

---

[4] There is, of course, nothing original in this thesis; and it would be disputed by some psychologists. But the above summary statement of it and of what seem to me good—and, indeed, obvious—reasons for accepting it, must, in the interest of brevity, suffice for the purpose of the present lecture.

radically different phenomena. We must therefore distinguish
—and the distinction is, I think, a fundamental but much
neglected one—between what we may call *terminal values*
and *adjectival values*.[5] Both have, or may have, present
valuedness, may be objects of present desire.

How different these two types of desire are may be seen
from the fact that the two may manifestly tend to opposite
courses of action. Victims of the Inquisition who did not
look forward to *post-mortem* rewards, had, obviously, no
desire to be burned at the stake; nevertheless, they also
presumably shrank from abjuring their actual beliefs and
of thinking of themselves as renegades or cowards; the
latter motive being the more powerful in them, they re-
fused to recant their heresy. On the other hand, the same
action may be prompted by either type of motive, or by one
re-enforcing the other. The consideration—to descend to a
less exalted example—that if I eat Welsh rabbit this evening,
I shall much regret it tomorrow, may not suffice to deter me
from the eating—if I like welsh-rabbit. But the addition of

[5] Since the above was written I have, through the courtesy of
Dr. John C. Whitehorn, formerly Director of the Department of
Psychiatry in The Johns Hopkins Medical School, received a
copy of a striking address delivered by him in 1951, in which
he recognizes clearly the distinction between what I have called
adjectival and terminal values, which he expressed by the terms
"the desire for roles" and "the desire for goals." "Human beings set patterns for themselves, they formulate roles. . . . To
perform skilled acts, to be a charming hostess, or a genial host,
or a high-pressure salesman, or a scholar and a gentleman—such
roles appear to outrank in value, to many, the attainment of the
practical *goals* toward which such patterns appear to be directed. . . . Many psychiatrists . . . have become accustomed to

the consideration that those who obtain trivial present pleasure at the cost of future pain are gluttonous fools, or weak-minded, may suffice to turn the scale in favor of abstinence.

These two types of motivation, then—the desire for *ends of action* and the desire for *qualities or adjectives as agent* —are irreducible to one another, and are in constant interplay in the inner experience of man and in the determination of his voluntary acts. There is no reason to assume the latter is never the more powerful; on the contrary, there is much evidence to show that it *is* usually the more powerful.

With the preceding distinctions made explicit, it is now possible to state unambiguously the meaning of the further general question: How does self-consciousness affect desire and choice? That question, upon the assumptions which have been laid down, now means for us this: What ideas pertinent to the possible action of an individual have their pleasantness or unpleasantness conditioned for him by the fact that he is self-conscious?

Now there are two essentially different ways in which the object-self may be conceived by the subject-self—the "Me"

---

think of the id as the source of all psychic energy. Yet the 'it' may rival or exceed the id, in the sense that being 'it' in one's preferred social role may become the principal mainspring of motivation. . . . Patterns of self-dramatization form the warp and woof of the texture of daily living." The antithesis of "roles" and "goals" is so neat that I should be tempted to substitute it for my own clumsier terminology, but for two principal considerations: (a) The word "roles" does not seem to cover the negative counterpart of the object of desire—the unpleasing picture of oneself, which evokes aversion and is at least a not less by the "I." It may, namely, be conceived as (1) a potential enjoyer of satisfactions or avoider of dissatisfactions, or (2) as a desirer or chooser of ends or a potential performer of acts. It is upon the peculiar desires conditioned by the second form of self-consciousness that I chiefly wish to dwell; but something should be said about the former. In this, the satisfactions in question may be of any sort under heaven, or above it. Actions which are in fact directed towards some such satisfactions are, of course, not necessarily accompanied by any explicit self-reference; they may be simply "drives." Seeking food when hungry may be a wholly un-self-conscious act. It eventuates in a satisfactory future experience of the self, but it is the response to an organic urge which may, and in the lower animals presumably does, operate without the aid of any distinction between self and nonself—being in this respect entirely similar to those urges which do *not* terminate in future satisfactions, such as the self-destructive impulse of the lemmings or the impulse of the mother-bird to draw predatory animals away from the nest at the risk of her own life. But when the idea of self supervenes upon the original or

potent factor in behavior; (b) "roles" and "goals" does not sharply indicate the potentially different relations, both temporal and qualitative, of the two types of desire to the real determinant of choice at the moment of decision. A "role" may, it is true, also become a "goal," i.e., be anticipated as about to be pleasurable when carried out; but it need not be, and may be the opposite, e.g., the role of martyr or of leader of a forlorn hope in battle. Dr. Whitehorn's address, "Social Psychodynamics," has been published in *The Journal of Psychiatric Social Work*, vol. 21, p. 2 ff.

acquired outfit of impulses, it profoundly modifies their action and may completely suppress some of them; and the first way in which it does so is by giving a special potency to those impulses or desires which *are* recognized as tending to eventuate in a future satisfaction of the object-self, and diminishing or destroying the potency of those which do not so eventuate. In short, it makes man capable of what is called deliberate selfishness—that is, of valuing ends because it is his own objective-self that will be the possessor or enjoyer of them, and it tends to deprive other ends of subjective value, that is, of present appeal to the subject-self.

It has, it is true, been denied by some psychologists, and notably by William James, that the mere first personal pronoun or pronominal adjective has this power to give to ends a desirableness which they would not otherwise possess or to rob others of an appeal, a present pleasantness, which they otherwise would possess. The pronoun "Me," it is said, is an abstraction. The "I" values things as good, "instinctively" or otherwise, and the things that it values it then, and therefore, calls "my" goods. But this view is, I think, contradicted by the evidence of experience. The first personal pronoun does have at times a strange value-enhancing or value-minimizing efficacy. For it is a notorious fact that in some persons it counteracts the most powerful primary impulses. I refer especially to those which, though biologically useful, that is, favorable to the preservation of the species, are known not to be conducive to the future satisfaction of the individual. Men do sometimes ask, with respect to propensions of this kind, "What after all do *I* get out of it?" And when they conclude that the object-self will get nothing out of it, they often enough repress their so-called "natural" inclinations, i.e., those which would be natural if men were devoid of self-consciousness. I do not say that this always or even usually happens; and I do not here discuss whether or how far, it is good that it should happen. But nothing seems more obvious than that calculations of self-interest—of what will satisfy the object-self conceived as an enjoyer—occur, and are, *as such*, more or less effective in the determination of behavior; the entire history of hedonistic ethics is a part of the evidence on the issue. A crucial instance may be seen in the belief in reincarnation. The Hindu is apparently more concerned about the condition in which he will be reborn than about the future rebirths of others. Why—since there is not assumed by him to be any continuous awareness of personal identity from one birth to another? Solely, it would appear, because he has learned to *call* one among the innumerable beings who will be born in the future "Me." It is about the fate of this one that he is peculiarly interested simply because the first personal pronoun is supposed to be in some sense applicable to it, and not to the others.

Yet though the self-conscious animal, looking upon the "Me" as a possible experiencer of satisfactions, thereby becomes capable of egoism in a sense in which no other animal is, he by the same process acquires certain other peculiar potencies which have, or may have, a contrary tendency. For, in the first place, the concept "myself" is meaningless except in contrast with "not-myself"; it implies at least a potential "other." And in its genesis, according to a theory held by some, the consciousness of self was the result of the prior discovery of an other. One form of this theory would make the awareness of self arise through the shock of opposition. A creature which encountered no resistance, which lived in a world where it had everything its own way, would perhaps never have the antithesis of self and not-self forced upon its attention. If this were sufficient to generate self-consciousness, we should have to ascribe that attribute to the animals; and it may be that, *in* this sense, they have a rudimentary and passing awareness of the antithesis, whenever they encounter obstacles, pain-causing objects, or enemies. But this is plainly not sufficient to account for the form which the contrast of self and not-self takes in man. If we must have a theory of the genesis of self-consciousness in him, the most plausible is that suggested in variant forms by Clifford, Royce, Baldwin, and others; that the infant becomes conscious of himself as a definite object of reference by first becoming aware—perhaps through imitation of their actions, and the discovery of the inner "feel" of those actions—that there are other beings who have feelings like his own, and then discovering that he and his experiences are objects for them, that they think of him—the so-called theory of the self as a "secondary eject." I cannot avoid some suspicion of a certain logical circularity in this genetic explanation; some self-consciousness seems to be already assumed in the very process by which its origination is explained; and in any case, it is of the nature of really genetic theories *not* to explain. If the thing to be accounted for is truly something new, an "emergent" or pure "mutation," then, though the theory may correctly describe the circumstances preceding or attending its emergence, it cannot deduce the necessity of its emerging from those circumstances. But at all events, it is patent that in man the "other" which gives meaning by contrast to the notion of the self does in fact consist chiefly of other persons, conceived as similar to the "Me," and conceived also as having the "Me"—what we may call "Me number one"—as an object of their thought and feeling; and Hegel does not greatly exaggerate when he writes in the *Phenomenology* that "self-consciousness exists in itself and for itself, in that, and by the fact that, it exists for another self-consciousness."

The makeshift polar counterpart of "the Me," then, being for man largely other selves, assumed to have the sort of experiences that he has, *his* self-consciousness implies that there are many other potential enjoyers of satisfactions. The effects of this upon his emotions and desires are complex and various; but in view of what has already been said of the determination of desire, one effect is that he may desire, i.e., take pleasure in the idea of, the enjoyment of satisfactions by others; and it is, I suggest, a fact of universal experience that this frequently occurs. Eighteenth-century moralists used to discuss at much length whether such desires could be called "disinterested." The distinctions already indicated make the answer easy; it is usually, if not always, the pleasantness of the idea of others' satisfaction to the subject-self of the moment, the present interest of the I, that determines the desire; but the pleasant idea in these cases is not that of the satisfaction of the "Me"; and this *is* disinterestedness in the only psychologically admissible sense of the term.

Man, then, by virtue of the other-consciousness which is deeply interwoven with his self-consciousness, is an animal aware of the fact that there are others "having insides *of* their own," though like *his* own; and this, so far as we have any means of judging, is not true of any other animal. It is apparently one of the biological differentiae of his species, which certainly affects his desires and therefore his behavior, though with astonishing individual variations in the degree in which it does so, and on the whole much less than one might have expected and might wish that it did. That, on balance, the two associated affective consequences of self-consciousness which we have thus far noted make the concrete behavior of men more serviceable to the well-being of others of their own kind, and—aside from other factors —more favorable to the survival of the species, is at least extremely questionable.

2

It may, then, serve to clarify our historical survey if we indicate certain further distinctions. These, when expressed, may seem very obvious; nevertheless, both our seventeenth and eighteenth century analysts of human nature and, I think, some very recent psychologists, do not always keep them clearly in mind. Under certain common generic names many of the older writers tended to confuse several affective phenomena which, though they are certainly closely related and perhaps rarely present in isolation, are by no means identical. We need not, at this point, attempt any adequate

analysis of the nature and interconnections of the familiar
types of experience which we are distinguishing. For the
present, our main concern is to discriminate these types
sufficiently for purposes of identification, when we encounter references to them in the texts; to provide them
with convenient names; and to intimate, by way of prelude,
some of the aspects of them which seem significant for the
general theory of man.

i.   First, then, is that peculiarity of man which consists
in a *susceptibility to pleasure in, or a desire for, the thought
of oneself as an object of thoughts or feelings, of certain
kinds, on the part of other persons.* Of this, three varieties
or degrees, at least, may be distinguished. There is (a) as
the minimal form of it, the mere wish to be "noticed," to be
at least an object of attention and interest on the part of
others. There is (b) the desire for affective attitudes—sympathy, friendliness, affection, love—which are not conceived
as necessarily equivalent to appraisals, to value-judgments
about us, though such attitudes may or may not in fact, in
the minds of the others, be conditioned by such judgments.
Children, it is to be hoped, usually have an affection for
their parents, however little they may approve of them.
There is (c) the desire for some form or degree of what is
called a "good opinion" of oneself on the part of other men.
What is desired in this last case by A, the subject, is usually
a state of feeling, but not *simply* a state of feeling, in B, the
other fellow, about A. The thought that A wants B to have
about him is a favorable *judgment,* and there is implicit in
the desire, therefore, the notion of truth or falsity, since that
is always implicit in the idea of a judgment. B's appraisal

of A, in short, may be true or false, either because B does not know the relevant facts about A or because he applies a wrong standard of valuation; we are all acquainted with people who complain that they have been "misjudged." The ways of thinking or feeling about us—about our qualities or acts or characters—which are desired on the part of others manifestly range through a scale of degrees which our common vocabulary roughly distinguishes: notice, interest, approval, respect, consideration, esteem, praise, admiration, applause, honor, veneration. These all, equally obviously, have their negative counterparts, running from mere indifference to contempt, which are correspondingly objects of aversion—supposed states of others' minds towards the self, the thought of which is to it, in differing degrees, unpleasant and repellent—though the negative counterpart of the least pleasurable of the positive series is, rather notoriously, usually the most unpleasurable; to be in a society and not to be noticed at all, to feel oneself not to be the object of anyone's interest or attention, seems to be, to most human creatures, most intolerable of all—a peculiarity which some have thought that dogs appear to share with us.

I have distinguished the three species of this genus of hedonic susceptibilities chiefly for the purpose of preventing confusion of the second with the third, which is the one pertinent to the subject of these lectures. Since it will be convenient to have a single name for this trait of man, we may steal one from the vocabulary of the now nearly extinct phrenologists, and call it "approbativeness"—using the word as a generic name for the several varieties or degrees of that desire which are listed in a "definition" of it in a phrenological text-book:

> Love of praise; desire to excel and be esteemed; ambition; desire to display and show off; . . . desire for a good name, for notoriety, fame . . . and to be well thought of, sensitiveness to the speeches of other people, and love of popularity.[6]

Two of the more obvious peculiarities of approbativeness may be noted in passing. Since the pleasure by which the desire is gratified attaches to the subject's belief about the thoughts of others about himself, that belief is manifestly extremely liable to arise from error or delusion—and, indeed, the desire is likely to generate error and delusion in proportion to its intensity, as the theological assailants and literary satirists of man's "pride" in the seventeenth and eighteenth centuries were disagreeably given to pointing out at length. It has also frequently been pointed out in later observations of this craving that it is variable with respect to the groups of others whose esteem or approbation is most desired—children notoriously often being far more concerned about the favorable opinions of schoolmates than of teachers or parents, criminals about that of their fellow-gangsters than of dull, law-abiding citizens, scholars about the "judgment of their peers" than of the *profanum vulgus*. These variables are in turn often subject to variations and reversals in the same person in different social *milieux;* a desire to enjoy, or to believe that one enjoys, the esteem or

---

[6] *The Self-Instructor in Phrenology and Physiology*, by O. S. and L. N. Fowler, reprint, 1899.

admiration of any company in which one at the moment happens to be, is apparently not uncommon, and since the criteria of the admirable in different *milieux* are highly various, the individual having such a desire may be protean, exhibiting, so to say, different colorings, a distinct "personality," in each group in which he finds himself.

Our familiarity with this trait of human nature—I mean "approbativeness" in general—tends to make us overlook its strangeness as a biological phenomenon. Regarded as such, it is so strange that some behavioristic psychologists and others in our time have denied its existence, or at least profess to be themselves devoid of it, while still behaving in ways which would be unintelligible if it were absent. They —and other men—they declare, care only about what other creatures overtly and physically do to them; a society of robots, recognized as such, is, we are told, as satisfying as any other, provided they are harmless and serviceable robots. There are indeed, philosophers living, and teaching in great universities, who have maintained that the very terms "others' thoughts" or "others' feelings"—including, therefore, others' thoughts or feelings about us—are but meaningless sounds; though these same philosophers continue to write books and articles apparently designed to be read and agreed with by others; and they seem incomprehensibly to exhibit symptoms of dissatisfaction when disparaging adjectives are applied by others to these works. Since those who profess these views are learned and distinguished persons—though, if what they say were true, the word "distinguished" itself would have no meaning—I ought perhaps to examine the grounds offered for such opinions; but there is here no time for that, and—to speak in a way which would be discourteous only if it were applied, as it here is not, to those who admit that I am really thinking about them —there appear to me to be heights of silliness sometimes attained by philosophers which it is not very profitable to take time to discuss.[7]

For the purpose of these lectures, at any rate, I shall assume that "approbativeness" exists, and that it actuates men's behavior. But, as I have said, the tendency of some contemporaries to deny its existence may serve to suggest how great a biological anomaly it appears to be. An animal which has an urgent desire for a thought *of* a thought—and of a thought not its own—and whose action is profoundly affected by this type of desire, more profoundly and more pervasively than by any other, as some contemporaries and many of the older writers have held—that is man; and he is therefore a singular member of the animal kingdom. We shall find a number of the seventeenth and eighteenth century theories of human nature defining this as the differentia of man *par excellence,* on the side of his "passions," or springs of action, as distinguished from his degree of intelligence—the attribute that, for better or worse, sets him apart from all other species—the great point, or one of the great points, of discontinuity in nature, i.e., to put it in modern phrasing, of discontinuity in the modes of determination of the motion of matter—since a determinant of human be-

[7] I have, however, examined this one in "The Paradox of the Thinking Behaviorist," *Philosophical Review,* XXXI, 1922, pp. 135-147.

havior *is* a determinant of the motion of those material aggregates called human bodies.

Approbativeness is a type of desire that is wholly indeterminate with respect to the modes of behavior that may result from it. For it manifestly presupposes approbations and disapprobations; it is a human trait which is conditioned by another human trait—the habit characteristic, probably, of all individuals of the species, of passing judgments of approval, admiration, etc., and their opposites, upon the qualities or acts of other individuals. If, then, there can be said to be any "laws" of approbativeness—any verifiable generalizations, at least statistical generalizations, about the ways in which it works—they will (subject to certain qualifications) be secondary to the laws of approbation and admiration. The nature of the acts which the approbative individual performs will be determined by what the people whose esteem or admiration he desires do in fact esteem and admire. The study of the one phenomenon, then, ought to be—though it frequently is not—correlated with the study of the other. Now, the phenomena of approbation are extremely diverse, and there are some interesting questions about them concerning which differing opinions have been held—in the period which we are to consider, and in our own time. Historically, the human traits or acts approved or admired obviously vary in different peoples and cultures, and in different periods of the same culture, and in different classes in the same period. It is, of course, one of the important tasks of the historian of ideas to record the sequence of changes in what may be called the *approbata* and *admirata* in a given society. These will coincide largely, but by no means completely, with changes in the currently accepted moral codes, as embodied in the *mores*. The coincidence is incomplete, for one reason, among others, because admiration and simple approval do not differ merely in degree; they are often, possibly oftener than not, evoked by different objects. There are, I incline to think, instances of admiration which are spontaneous, essentially aesthetic responses in the individual to certain characteristics or modes of action in other men; and these responses may be out of accord with the ordinary moral criteria which the same individual accepts. Exceptional courage, strength of will, intellectual power, may evoke admiration independently of any moral approbation of the behavior in which they are manifested. The history of men's admirations would be largely a study of their heroes—the characters, actual or fictitious, who, in different periods, were in a high degree the objects of this feeling—with an attempt to determine what, in particular, in the heroes, aroused the feeling.

But to know the historical facts about men's approbations and admirations, and their changes, is the least difficult part of the business. There still remains the question of the causes or conditioning antecedents, of any given widely prevalent valuation of one type of human quality or character, and of the change from it to a quite different one. Why, under what influences, in connection with what other processes, did that valuation originate, and later give place, it may be, to its opposite?

It is, moreover, evident that approbation or admiration, and their opposites, are not primary, i.e., unanalyzable or irreducible, phenomena. For they, too, are attended by pleasantness or unpleasantness. People take pleasure in approving, admiring, applauding, idolizing others; they also take pleasure—frequently, as is notorious, a more intense pleasure—in disapproving, censuring, dispraising. Any of these mental acts may therefore be manifestations of something lying deeper—the desire to enjoy the pleasure attaching to them. And any such desire, in turn, may be a manifestation of some more general and fundamental hedonic susceptibility. The pleasure of approving and expressing approval, or its opposite, may be (I am not saying that it always is) due to the satisfaction which it affords the self-esteem, the sense of importance, or the feeling of superiority, of the approver (motives which we shall shortly consider more particularly). To approve, and still more to disapprove, is to sit in judgment on your fellows; and the rôle of judge is naturally a gratifying one. Now the approver or disapprover is also an *object* of approbation or disapprobation on the part of others; there are approbations of approbations and, indeed, of the approbational attitude in general. And John's approbation or disapprobation of James, *quâ* approver or disapprover, may be determined by his conjecture or suspicion as to James's underlying motive in mounting the judge's bench. If he believes that—especially in disapproving or condemning—James is gratifying his vanity or self-esteem or wish to think himself better than others, John is likely to disapprove James's attitude of disapprobation. But in doing so, he may be unconsciously actuated by fundamentally the same type of motive that he condemns in James. What are called censorious people, persons who disapprove too much, are not popular partly because it is suspected that they must take a malicious pleasure in a state of mind in which they so frequently indulge, but which runs counter to the approbative desires of other men. If, then, John wishes to be approved by James—and everybody else—he will restrain his own dissapprobative propensities. Approbativeness thus tends to impose checks on disapprobation—or at least on the manifestation of it—*through* disapprobation. Such are a few of the complex involutions arising from the fact that approbation or disapprobation may be directed on itself.

Approbation or disapprobation may likewise be directed upon approbativeness. A man, or a people, may be approved for manifesting "a decent respect to the opinions of mankind." On the other hand, if James believes that John's act is prompted merely by a desire for approbation—especially for some of its more extreme forms, admiration or applause or fame—he may disapprove, or at least fail to admire, John and his motive, even though he may welcome the act resulting from that motive. This tendency to disapprove of approbativeness is, however, very variable. It appears to be more characteristic of some peoples or cultures than others. Savages and some civilized peoples do not seem to think ill of a man for betraying the fact that he values and desires esteem, admiration, applause. Some among the ancient Greeks and Romans apparently regarded this desire as not only pardonable but laudable. Aristotle, for example, sets it down among the virtues, provided it be not exaggerated, that is, disproportionate to one's actual deserts. For what he calls μεγαλοψυχία (usually translated "greatness of soul" or "magnanimity") is expressly defined by him as "reaching out after esteem" or "honor"

($τιμή$). "He who thinks esteem a small thing, will think everything else a small thing," for it is the principal reason why other *desiderata* are desired. This kind of pride "appears to be a sort of crown [or ornament, $κόσμος$] of the virtues; it enhances them and cannot come into existence without them."[8] Aristotle, it is true, in his picture of the $μεγαλόψυχος$ frequently confuses approbativeness with self-esteem, so that it is sometimes impossible to be sure to which he is referring; what is pertinent here is the fact that he is far from condemning the former—or, in fact, either. Neither modesty nor the concealment of one's good deeds or qualities seems to have been usually counted by the Greeks among the virtues. Other examples of this from classical writers might be cited.[9]

In our own code, however, the tendency to disapprove of manifestations of approbativeness is a conspicuous feature, though with curious variations. It is a paradoxical and, I think, (if I may express a disapprobation of my own) a rather unfortunate development in human nature. For James's approbation becomes effective as an influence upon John's behavior through John's approbativeness. In so far, then, as approbativeness is disapproved, approbation works against itself, tends to weaken the force through which it functions. It is probably incapable of greatly weakening the subjective *desire;* but it forces that desire to conceal

[8] *Nicomachean Ethics*, II, 7; IV, 4.

[9] E.g., Euripides, *Medea*, 543-5: Jason exclaims: "May there be no gold in my house, nor may I sing strains more sweet than those of Orpheus, if it be my lot not to be distinguished [or applauded]." What he is apparently saying is that he would find no value either in wealth or in the highest artistic achievement, if neither gained public recognition.

itself and so gives rise to a vast deal of insincerity; and it
deprives that useful desire of some of its natural gratification. Disapprobation of approbativeness or of the candid
manifestation of it, ought, I suggest, to be disapproved; for
it springs from motives which, when recognized, *are* normally disapproved as unpleasing traits of human nature. It
is possible and desirable to take pleasure in the innocent
and unconcealed pleasure of another man in being praised.
We do not, for example, tend to disapprove the aversion
from, or fear of, disapprobation, but rather the desire of
approbation. But also, disapproval of the latter varies with
the nature of the acts or qualities for which approbation is
desired. It is less usually applied to the desire for admiration and praise for the successful public performance of
specific acts of skill; we do not condemn actors or opera-
singers for seeking applause, and we take pleasure in giving
it to them. It is the manifestation of a desire for approbation of what are usually distinguished as moral qualities
or acts that most commonly arouses disapprobation; and
though the motivation of this is certainly complex, it is
clearly due largely to a feeling that such approbativeness
itself is a morally unadmirable or even reprehensible
motive. This feeling has been insistently inculcated by
Christianity. "Take heed that ye do not your righteousness
before men, to be seen of them. . . . When thou givest alms,
let not thy left hand know what thy right doeth: that thine
alms may be in secret."

As a spring of action—a desire seeking satisfaction—it is,
in its more normal manifestations, not only obviously of the
greatest social utility, but also usually the object of social

approbation and admiration. For, in so far as its satisfaction is conditioned upon actual achievement, it is a potent incentive to the maximum exercise of the energies of the individual; if no one ever cared about reaching the head of the class, it is probable that classes—whether in schools or in the activities of later life—would show a much lower level of performance than they do. And those who are actuated by this desire, at least in certain of its forms, are, if I am not mistaken, generally more highly esteemed than those who do not. The pass-man in a college is not, I suppose, commonly more highly thought of than the honors man.

3

ii. It is, however, equally plainly characteristic of man that he likes not only to be well thought of but also to think well of himself; this trait—both the capacity for pleasure in, and the desire for, a pleasing idea of oneself— I shall call self-approbativeness, or the desire for self-esteem. In the older terminology, it is sometimes designated by the same names as approbativeness, the difference in the author's reference needing to be gathered from the context. The French *amour-propre,* and sometimes the English "self-love," and the now obsolete word "philauty" are also ambiguous; either may, in different writers or contexts, refer to the desire for individual pleasure or satisfaction of any kind, or to self-esteem exclusively.

In this type of experience the self as chooser or as actor

is conceived by itself as actually or potentially characterized in these capacities by certain adjectives or epithets—in other words, as possessing certain qualities—more or less irrespective of appraisals of it by others. It has, indeed, been questioned whether self-esteem is not a derivative from approbativeness, and whether some dim sense of a potential external approver is not always present in it. But I shall assume it to be a fact that it can exist without an explicit reference to any actual thought of others about oneself, so that one finds a present satisfaction simply in thinking that one is—or is about to be—the proper subject of favorable adjectives, or a present dissatisfaction—which is usually, I think, in most men more intense and more potent as a determinant of behavior than the corresponding satisfaction—in thinking of oneself as characterizable by disparaging or condemnatory adjectives.

Men, in short, obviously, have a peculiarly intense hedonic susceptibility to self-esteem and are moved in their conduct by a desire or need of it; some modest measure of it, at least, is probably—as much evidence from psychopathology tends to show—indispensable to endurable existence for creatures constituted as we are. It is the need which, in its pathological forms, generates "compensations" and delusions of grandeur.

The question of the relations of self-esteem to approbativeness is, however, not a simple one. They are manifestly closely related. Self-approbation is supported by the approbation of others; it is easier to feel satisfied with your qualities or your acts or performances if your fellows appear to think highly of them. On the other hand, self-esteem may take the form of an indifference to or contempt for the opinion of other persons, or of some classes or types of other persons. The individual esteems himself the more because he is, or believes himself to be, unconcerned about the esteem of his neighbors; and those who give alms in secret perhaps gain more in enhanced self-approval than they lose through the repression of their approbativeness. And whereas it is obvious that approbativeness tends in the main to compliance with social, that is, external, requirements and standards, the desire for self-esteem—in certain though by no means in all forms—may manifest itself outwardly in bumptiousness, aggressiveness, defiance of social conventions and rules. It is, in short, sometimes a revolt of the individual againt his own approbativeness, which he feels, puts him into a humiliating position of subjection to other men—that is, to their judgments or feelings about him. It is, in this form, an attainment which the Cynic and Stoic schools in antiquity conceived to be an essential part of moral excellence, exemplified best of all in the traditional pictures of Diogenes as a model of the supreme and godlike virtue of "self-sufficiency"; though, as Diogenes was also rather ostentatious about it, Plato and others, according to the familiar stories, intimated that his professed scorn of other men's opinions of him was only a way of "showing off."[10] To *proclaim* your freedom from approbativeness is plainly to manifest approbativeness—to make it evident that you wish to be admired by others for your indifference to

[10] *The Lives and Opinions of Eminent Philosophers*, by *Diogenes Laërtius*, C. D. Young translation, 1895, p. 226.

their admiration. I remember hearing an English public man, in a speech addressed to a group of Americans during World War I, boast that the English never boasted.

But though self-esteem—either the feeling of it or the desire for the feeling—*may* manifest itself in a disregard or defiance of socially current criteria of the approvable or admirable, it need not do so, and usually does not. The individual may, the average man does, accept those criteria, and find or seek to find his satisfaction in the belief that his qualities or performances conform to them in a sufficient, or in an unusual, degree—whatever others may think. When this is the case, the desire of self-esteem, not less than approbativeness, becomes a potent subjective enforcer of the *mores*. Or his self-esteem or disesteem may be not solely an echo of current valuations, but a return upon himself of his own spontaneous, quasi-aesthetic approbations or admirations of attributes which he has first observed in others, or of his spontaneous dislike or contempt of the opposite attributes, when he finds them in others. The desire to be like the persons one admires—or to be like them in that particular characteristic or potency which one admires in them—is certainly one of the most powerful springs of action, especially in the young.

For self-appraisal, whether favorable or unfavorable—and most of all, the appraisal, at the moment preceding choice, of alternative possible acts of one's own—is profoundly affected by the fact that every man is also an approver or disapprover of others. As he applies adjectives or epithets to them and their acts, so do they to him and his acts. And his need of some degree of self-esteem is thereby, as it were, caught in a trap—or, to change the figure, his approbations or disapprobations of his fellows are converted into boomerangs. For it is difficult to approve in oneself qualities or acts which one condemns and berates in others. Thus the desire to think well or at any rate, not to think too badly of oneself is a motive making for conformity to something analogous to the categorical imperative; the standards of approbation or disapprobation which the individual applies to himself, or to the contemplated courses of action to which other motives incline him, *tend* to be the same as those which he would apply to all human beings under similar circumstances. It is not, to be sure, true that they invariably are. An individual's need for self-esteem also often begets great ingenuity in finding reasons for thinking his own case exceptional; and some people's serene unconsciousness of faults in themselves which they violently censure in their neighbors is one of the familiar themes of comedy. Yet in the main, I think, the working of this desire *is* controlled by a simple logic of consistency—by the rule of judging of yourself as you would judge of others. It is not that men, in general, consciously adopt such a rule as a moral imperative, but that they cannot wholly avoid acting in accordance with it; and when they fail to do so, their fellows are usually quick to point out the inconsistency. Thus, though the desire to have a favorable opinion of one's own behavior or performances is undeniably, in a sense an egoistic or self-regarding motive it is capable of counteracting all other self-regarding motives, and of introducing a kind of impersonality into the determination of the action of individuals. It is a sort of desire which is inevitably entangled with the first ingredient of rationality or logicality—the formal principle of self-consistency. Nor, evidently, is it merely the *form* of reasonableness that naturally becomes associated with this desire; the specific *content* or criterion of self-appraisal also tends to become depersonalized. James, as approver or disapprover of John, is unlikely to approve of conduct by John which causes pain or injury to himself, James; and since he is also an approver or disapprover of himself, and since his self-judgments—or his judgments of future actions which he might perform—normally consist in applying to these the same adjectives which the same *kinds* of qualities or acts on John's part habitually evoke in him, it is—in so far as the desire of self-approbation is actually influencing his choice—difficult for him to think well of himself as causing pain to John. The difficulty, unhappily, is by no means an impossibility, partly because the self-approbative desire may be overcome by others, partly because self-esteem, once more, is fertile in suggesting sophistical reasons—in short, "rationalization"—for differentiating the case of John from his own case, and so for gratifying without self-reproach his inclination to actions which may be injurious to John. Nevertheless, the desire for self-esteem does—among its very diverse effects—exercise a pressure upon the individual towards conformity with the rule: Do unto others as ye would that they should do unto you. The question: "What would you think of me if I did to you the sort of thing that you are doing to me?" is always a hard challenge to meet; but it is an appeal which gets its potency from the desire for self-approval of the person to whom it is addressed.

There is, moreover, as I indicated earlier,[11] a yet more essential relation between self-approbativeness and morality —by which term I here mean, not good or desirable overt behavior, but a certain type of subjective experience, apparently peculiar to man. Though anyone is free, of course, to define the word "moral" as he likes, there is a sense— and, I think, the most appropriate and useful sense—of the word in which it may be said that it is by virtue of the desire for approbative—or nondisapprobative—adjectival values for his acts or qualities that man is a moral agent. For that type of experience which would generally be called "moral" (in the descriptive, not the eulogistic sense) certainly does not consist simply in being aware that the desire for one potentially realizable terminal value is stronger than the desire for another. The distinguishing fact about this sort of experience is that it requires a special verb for its expression—the verb "ought," with the first personal pronoun for its subject. And those who use this expression obviously do *not* mean by it merely "I desire."

It is to be noted that, like approbativeness, the craving for self-esteem or aversion from self-disesteem seems a biological singularity. Though we have little, if any, real knowledge of the subjective life of other organisms, we have no reason to suppose that they are what men certainly are —desirers and fearers of adjectives. This desire, together

[11] In an article "Terminal and Adjectival Values" in *The Journal of Philosophy*, vol. XLVII, p. 593 ff., from which part of the above is taken.

with approbativeness, is the most conspicuous manifestation in our appetitive life of what is, to all appearance, the great chasm in the organic world—the chasm between simply conscious and self-conscious animals. But it is at least clear that between a creature which simply feels, perceives, acts, and one which has come to form an idea of *itself* as a distinct entity *that* feels, perceives, acts, there cannot but be a profound difference. For by virtue of his self-consciousness man is divided within and against himself; every man, in so far as he experiences this mode of consciousness, has in a sense—though not necessarily in the psychopathologist's sense—a split personality. He has a complex mass of instincts, appetites, drives, desires, potentialities, feelings, emotions, attitudes, which make up what, at any given moment, he primarily *is;* but he is also capable, at least at other moments, of taking the attitude of external observer towards all of these, of looker-on at the very process of his own experience, and at himself as the experiencer or the doer of it all. He is in short, both actor and spectator, both performer and commentator on or critic of the performance. It is doubtless true, as some psychologists have insisted, that the spectator is never totally identical with the actor, at the same instant. His concrete momentary personality, when he is conscious of himself, includes components—e.g., certain feelings —of which he is not at the same time fully self-conscious. There is validity in the distinction between the subjective self of the moment, which is thinking, or *is* the thinking, and the objectified self which is being thought about—between (in William James's terms) the I and the Me. Nevertheless, the very essence of the experience is a judgment of identification of the two; the subject, or I, says to itself: this Me, this being that I am thinking about, is nevertheless in some sense and in some degree the same as the present, living, conscious I who am now thinking about it. The word "Me" is still simply the objective case of the first personal pronoun. Without this assumption of identity the emotions connected with self-consciousness would lose all their poignancy.

In any properly systematic theory of human nature man's self-consciousness would be recognized as a pervasive factor with which all the rest should be correlated. The instincts and propensities which constitute our heritage from our animal ancestors, and all the primary emotive and appetitive states of consciousness and their combinations would, of course, be explored and discriminated; but the questions constantly asked would be: how do they interact with, how are they modified or transformed by, self-consciousness, and what emotions and desires are there in man which could not conceivably exist at all if he were not self-conscious? That self-consciousness *is,* so far as we can judge, the principle differentia of the species man, and is in any case the central fact which should control any well-ordered investigation of his nature and behavior, has not, so far as my reading goes, been at all generally realized by psychologists; but a growing appreciation of it is evident in the more recent literature on the subject. William James, who was not only a psychologist but also—what is by no means a synonymous expression—acquainted with human nature, was well aware of it; and it has been well emphasized by (among others) McDougall in his *Social Psy-*

chology, by Hocking in his *Human Nature and its Remaking,* and by Edman in his *Human Traits.* But books purporting to tell us about human nature, in which its fundamental generic peculiarity is not so much as mentioned, continue to be published and apparently to be eagerly purchased by the general public. Editions of *Hamlet* with Hamlet left out still flood the bookstores.

It must not, however, be supposed that self-consciousness as such *accounts for* the emotions and desires that are conditioned by it and associated with it—such as self-esteem and approbativeness. It is, no doubt, conceivable that man might have been a spectator of himself without being an applauding or a critical spectator—might have been simply a detached and disinterested looker-on at the spectacle of his own life; and it appears to have been the opinion of Mr. George Santayana that he can and should be. I may venture to add that diligent reading of nearly all of the philosophical writings of Santayana, who had an acute mind, has not left me with the impression that he was wholly unaware that he wrote in an original and brilliant style or that he took no pleasure in doing so, or that he did not intend or expect to affect the opinions and the physical behavior of others by the publication of his books—at least to cause the physical act of purchasing the books. But for the purposes of the student of man as he actually is, it is enough to accept the empirical fact that the self-conscious animal has certain unique emotional susceptibilities and desires and potentialities, and to note what these are, what their subspecies or derivatives are, and what sorts of external effects they produce. And, as it happens, it was in these questions that the writers of the seventeenth and eighteenth centuries with whom we shall later deal were especially interested. They were mainly exploring, or trying to explore, the realm of the desires of men *quâ* self-conscious. They were not, it is true, always, or usually, aware that this was what they were doing. But the fact that they *were* doing it is what gives the preceding remarks their special relevance to the historical lectures that are to follow; for we shall now be able to have in mind the relation between the various particular reflections on men's motives which will be cited, and the general and distinguishing feature of the human constitution to which they are implicitly pertinent.

An individual's manifestation, in speech and manner, not of the desire for self-esteem but of the gratifying self-appraisal in which the desire finds its satisfaction, is, at least in our own *mores,* more generally and severely reprobated and repressed by one's fellows than are the manifestations of his approbativeness. Since his outward behavior is, nevertheless, powerfully influenced by his approbativeness, there is in him often a concealed conflict between the two desires —his approbativeness and his urge to give expression to his self-esteem or his pride in his qualities or achievements or possessions. This conflict seems to be especially acute in childhood and early adolescence, partly because one's fellows of that age are, especially in some cultures, even more zealous and severe in repressing the latter propensity than are parents and teachers. English schoolboys are ruthless in their treatment of any boy who seems to them to be given to "swank." In the end, i.e., in the adult, the de-

sire for social approbation, which can be obtained only by
the suppression or the concealment of self-approbation or
self-admiration, usually proves somewhat the stronger,
though the degree of its preponderance varies widely with
differences of early education, of the established rules of
social intercourse in particular societies, and, within a
society, of social classes. Whatever the means employed
for repressing the outward manifestation of pride, and in
spite of great variations and limitations of their potency,
they manifestly have in a modern society considerable influence upon conduct. If you wish to conform to the accepted code, you must refer modestly, if at all, to yourself
and your accomplishments and your belongings, and must
deprecate the admiration and praise of these by others.
"Ostentatious" is not a complimentary adjective. Yet,
though the expression of pride, as of approbativeness, may
be repressed, the inner feeling is not necessarily, or, it may
be suspected, usually, thereby extinguished or even diminished; such, at least, as we shall see, was the opinion—or
the confession—of some seventeenth- and eighteenth-century
writers. In short, the effect of the conjunction in human
nature of approbativeness with the propensity to self-esteem, and of the adverse impact of the former upon the
manifestation of the latter, has been to produce a large
amount of self-concealment and of insincerity in the average individual's intercourse with other members of his
social group. He is expected to pay compliments to them,
and often does so even though he may think the compliments excessive or unmerited; he is expected not to pay
compliments to himself, even though he may think, and

perhaps justly think, that he deserves them. (In the Society
of Friends, the former at least, I take it, is not expected or
approved, since it is inconsistent with "plain speech.")
Complete candor, in either respect, is hardly compatible
with what is generally regarded as approvable social behavior. This may seem an unhappy consequence of the interplay of the two desires of self-conscious beings which
we have been considering. But it is an actual and, human
nature being what it is, perhaps not a wholly regrettable
consequence. The two rules of the game (as we may call
them) which I have just mentioned—praise others, don't
praise yourself—probably serve to increase the total sum
of pleasure enjoyed by the participants in social converse.
The first rule does so obviously; the second, though it
demands the repression of a strong natural propensity, may
provide a compensation for this by a heightening of the
individual's *unexpressed* self-esteem, arising from his sense
of conforming to a generally approved requirement, which
he himself approves when it is applied to others. Let me
add that these latter observations must not be construed as
implying a cynical view of all the motivations in ordinary
social intercourse—though we shall find such a view expressed by some seventeenth- and eighteenth-century commentators on human nature. There certainly occur in man's
emotional life (as I have already said) such things as
genuine and intensely felt approbations and admirations
of the qualities, motives, or actions of others, and there is
a lively pleasure simply in giving such feelings expression
—in bestowing praise. And there are some minds (not too
numerous) who, without being oblivious of others' faults or

weaknesses, have a genius for discerning, in the very mixed complexes of qualities and motives that diversely characterize their fellows, the *right things* to praise. One could wish such minds more numerous. For it would appear that a social and self-conscious creature has an organic need of "appreciation" i.e., of praise, and would find existence almost insupportable without ever receiving any; but it also is necessary that praise be directed upon, and solely upon, what is (as Adam Smith would have said) in fact "praiseworthy." But what this is I shall not here attempt to say; for that is a large question of ethics, and we are not in this lecture primarily concerned with ethics but with an inquiry into human nature—not what man ought to be but what he is.

4

iii.   There is a further type of desire—a variant form of the two thus far mentioned—which had a conspicuous place in seventeenth- and eighteenth-century theories of human nature and is receiving a good deal of attention in our own time—what is called the desire for superiority, or for the feeling of superiority; we shall name it, for the sake of brevity, emulativeness. Its negative counterpart, the aversion from the gnawing feeling of inferiority, plays a dominating part in the psychology and psychopathology of Alfred Adler and his school, whose ideas have been taken up by numerous biographers, historians, and novelists, and have become a part of the current popular psychology. Let us first note some of the diverse effects of this subjective ingredient of human nature.

The nature of those effects will, of course, depend upon the nature of the quality or power or status in which the subject finds pleasure in believing himself superior to others. Attitudes and behavior the reverse of aggressive may be associated with, and even be motivated by, this feeling. The Stoic philosopher, the saint, or the Quaker, who submit to persecution without resistance, may—it is sometimes evident from their utterances that they do—feel themselves superior to their persecutors precisely because they do *not* resist; the Indian followers of Gandhi, it may plausibly be conjectured, had at least a gentle scorn for the spiritual crudity of the Western barbarians to whose physical power they outwardly submitted. The analysts of human motives who like to dwell especially upon this trait have been wont to point out that pride in one's pacific spirit, as in one's modesty or humility, may sometimes be the last refuge, and one of the more intense forms, of the sense of superiority.

Nor is the emulative desire for individual distinction among one's fellows inevitably or usually an exacting one. Hobbes, indeed, thought otherwise; "glory," he wrote, "consisteth in comparison and precellence," and therefore "if all men have it, no man hath it"—an observation wittily versified by W. S. Gilbert in the song in *The Gondoliers* which relates the disappointing experience of the too kindhearted king who, aware of the universality of this passion,

To the top of every tree
Promoted everybody,

only to discover that he had rather diminished than increased the happiness of his subjects, since

> When everybody's somebody,
> Then no one's anybody.

The difficulty of generally gratifying this desire is not, however, really so great as this implies. Though not everyone can occupy the top of every tree, there are, in fact, many trees, and the emulativeness of the average man seems fairly satisfied if he can promote himself, at all events in his own mind, to the top of one, or a few, and those not necessarily the highest; the most essential thing—so far as this appetency is concerned—apparently is, not that there shall be none higher but, at any rate, some lower, "with whom comparing" (in Hobbes's phrase) "the mind may find *somewhat* wherein to triumph and vaunt itself." What are its relations to approbativeness and self-esteem? The term "desire for superiority" appears to cover several complex psychic states which need to be distinguished, primarily with reference to the nature of the desired objects or states-of-things. It may designate simply the comparative modes of approbativeness or of self-esteem. Both of these desires naturally tend to take that form because social approbations are so largely comparative. We are forever engaged in ranking people: "Mr. Jones is a more public-spirited citizen than Mr. Smith," "Shakespeare is a greater dramatist than Ben Jonson." The desire to be well thought of, or to think well of oneself, thus passes over into the desire to be thought, or to think oneself, better than somebody else, in some respect or other. But the desire for, or the agreeable feeling of, superiority, in this sense, may exist without any unfriendly emotion or aggressive attitude towards others. A temperate man who pleasurably regards himself as superior to his too bibulous neighbor does not usually proceed to injure the drunkard, towards whom he may have the kindliest feeling. Simple emulation has nothing necessarily antisocial about it, but is obviously, on the contrary, of high social utility. When directed upon actual superiority in qualities or performances that are socially valued, and especially when it at the same time takes the form of a settled *conviction* of superiority, or of membership in a superior class, it may produce, not merely conformity to the accepted mores, but behavior excelling in disinterestedness and in social utility their ordinary requirements—"action above and beyond the call of duty," as the Army terms it. The individual becomes incapable of thinking of himself as acting in ways in which the generality of men act without social reprobation. The cultivation of *esprit de corps* consists largely in generating in individuals a sense of belonging to a class of persons for whom the common levels of excellence—in whatever kind of activity the group may be distinctively concerned—are insufficient to justify self-respect: *"la Garde meurt, mais ne se rend pas"*—not, be it noted, *"doit mourir."*

Undeniably, however, emulation takes on much less innocuous or useful forms. The desire to feel oneself superior finds its easiest gratification, not in the achievement of some superiority in fact, but in the disparagement of the qualities or achievements of others, which forms so large and agreeable a part of social conversation, sometimes even in academic circles. And it tends to ally itself with various other and more primitive elements of human nature—with the sadistic strain from which few men are completely free, though in most it is, happily, repressed or sublimated, with acquisitiveness, with pugnacity. In one of its modes it is akin to approbativeness, that is, is another species of the same genus—a desire for the thought of a thought in the consciousness of others. And approbativeness, though itself a hedonic susceptibility making chiefly for compliance and amicable social relations, may by degrees shade off into the most antisocial form of emulation. For the pleasant idea of being highly thought of, or admired, by others, is not extremely remote from the idea of being feared by them—fear being a recognition of a kind of superiority, and sometimes having an element of reluctant admiration in it. The aggressive behavior of individuals, or of nations, may therefore be prompted, at least in part, by a desire to extort from others a recognition of the superior excellence which the individaul or nation imputes to itself. This transformation of emulative approbativeness, *plus* unsatisfied self-esteem, seems to me to have had at least as great a part in producing the present condition of mankind as the class of factors usually called economic—that is, the desires for a particular sort of terminal values.

The reason for recalling such familiar facts about human nature as these is that the *diversity* of the propensities and modes of behavior springing, under differing conditions, from a common root has not always been recognized. Some writers—Hobbes, for example—have been curiously oblivious of the more desirable effects which the emulative "pas-

sion of glory" can produce; for him it was merely a "cause
of quarrel" amongst men. Others, oversimplifying in the
opposite way, have dwelt almost exclusively upon its happier manifestations. And not many have given much consideration to the question, under what conditions emulation assumes one form or the other, or to the question as to
its interactions with approbativeness and with what I have
called the boomerang-effect of approbation or disapprobation acting upon self-esteem. In a fairly close and homo-
geneous society, these last two forces operate very potently
to diminish or repress the antisocial, or generally disliked,
methods of gratifying the emulative form of self-esteem.
But that desire is too intense and persistent to be wholly
extirpated.

5

iv. However much comparative self-esteem—the feeling of superiority—and the sort of behavior in which it
manifests itself, may be repressed and frustrated in the individual in his relations with other individuals of his immediate socal group, it can, and often does, reassert itself in
a collective form—in what the late A. Clutton-Brock aptly
called "pooled self-esteem"[12]—above all, as this is exhibited
in the behavior of nations towards other nations. When we
observe it in a people not our own we call it chauvinism.

[12] In an essay by that title first published in *The Atlantic
Monthly*, December, 1921.

You will *not* be approved by most of your countrymen if you publicly express the opinion that your, and their, national group—its qualities and institutions and ways of living and type of culture—are inferior to those of most, or even of some, other countries; and national anthems (so far as I am acquainted with them) are usually uninhibited outbursts of collective self-glorification. However, the pooled form of the feeling of superiority, though it obviously must usually be irrational and absurd, would be relatively harmless if its expression were confined to speech and song at home. But it is not so confined; and it always tends to produce international ill feeling, and frequently—given the hope of military success—the launching of an international war.

In particular, pooled self-esteem is the trait in human nature which has played the greatest and most disastrous part in the history of mankind in the first half of the twentieth century. But Clutton-Brock's essay of 1921 was (so far as I have noted) the first, and is, I think, a partially successful attempt to analyze and explain it. Since the essay is apparently not well known, I am tempted to incorporate the greater part of it in this lecture. That, however, is not possible. But I cannot forebear to summarize the principal observations contained in it, partly in my own, partly in its author's words. He not unjustly, I think, reproached contemporary psychology for its failure to study adequately, or for the most part, even seriously, this phenomenon—the desire of men to think highly of themselves, Hobbes's "passion of glory," even aside from its "pooled" form. The reproach was more justified when he wrote than it is now; but it can still be laid against much pretentiously "scientific" psychology. The immense rôle which this type of motivation plays in all provinces of behavior is still insufficiently recognized and investigated by the general psychologists, though the psychopathologists, being, by the nature of their profession, compelled to face the facts more fully and directly, have been duly mindful of it. "What a vast part of us," Clutton-Brock wrote, "is just vanity—far vaster than the part that is instinct and appetite." This last clause, in particular—though it is probably, for most psychologists, heterodox—seems to me to be only a little exaggerated.

But it was with the special form which this motive took in men as members of those organized social groups called nations that Clutton-Brock was chiefly concerned. What he pointed out was that the sort of disapprobation by others which plays the largest part in repressing the propensities in human nature potentially dangerous to social order and harmony is usually impotent in individuals when conceiving of themselves as citizens of a State; and—a fact more pregnant and more disquieting still—that, in that phase of the self-consciousness of the average individual, these same propensities not only find a new haven, but show an intensification arising from their very repression in other parts of his life. Dr. Jonson's definition of patriotism needs amendment. Patriotism is not necessarily or usually "the last refuge of a scoundrel"; but much that goes by the name *is* the last refuge of the scoundrel-strains in the minds of millions of men most of whom, in the other relations of life, are probably not scoundrels—the strains of unsatisfied vanity, the desire to brag and "show off," the pleasure of thinking ill of other men, envy, the lust to dominate, and those latent destructive and sadistic tendencies which are usually repressed or sublimated to relatively harmless forms within the group. All these impulses are much too tenacious ingredients of that strange complex which we call human nature to be readily or completely extirpated. Prevented from expressing themselves in one way, they seek another. And they most easily find it when the individual thinks of himself as a citizen of a state *vis-à-vis* other states. It is also the strain in the average man's make-up of which the ambitious demagogue, seeking political prestige and power for himself, most easily and effectively can, and usually does, take advantage.

Clutton-Brock apparently believed the conversion of self-esteem and the desire for a sense of superiority into a pooled form to be especially characteristic of our own age, as a result of the development of machine-production. The average wage-earner spends his days in the endless repetition of simple, uninteresting, mechanical tasks, from which he can gain no gratifying sense of personal achievement. "In all industrial societies, the vast majority never find a scope for the full exercise of their faculties, and are aware of their inferiority to the successful few." But emphasis upon this as a major causal factor seems to me an error. Pooled self-esteem flourished long before the Industrial Revolution, though it had less ruinous effects because weapons were less destructive; and in our own time it has not been the industrial working-classes who have most conspicuously manifested the pathological symptoms of it—e.g., in Germany in the decades from 1872 to 1914.

The workers were mainly preoccupied with the pursuit of terminal values of their own—higher wages, better housing, better working conditions. There are, however, two other reasons recognized by Clutton-Brock why self-esteem and emulation tend—doubtless, in some degree, in nearly all classes of a national group—to be pooled. One is that vanity in its individual form is not usually encouraged but frustrated by the other members of the group; the other is that, in its pooled form, it *is* encouraged, because it is shared, by them. As Clutton-Brock observes,

it becomes impossible for me to believe that I am such a wonder as I should like to think myself, in the face of surrounding incredulity; so I seek for something, seeming to be not myself, that I can believe to be a wonder, without arousing criticism and incredulity; in fact, something which others also believe to be a wonder, because it seems to them not to be themselves. There are many such things, but the largest, the most convincing, and the most generally believed in is Our Country. . . . What we need, and what we get, is a something which at the same time distinguishes us from a great part of the human race, and yet is shared by nearly all those with whom we come in contact. That we find in our country; and in our country we do most successfully and unconsciously pool our self-esteem. So no league of nations, no polite speeches of kings and presidents, . . . will keep us from hating each other and feeling good when we do so, unless we can attain to enough self-knowledge to understand why it is that we hate each other, and to see that this mutual hate and boasting are but a suppressed and far more dangerous form of that vanity which we have learned, at least, not to betray in our personal relations.[13]

Clutton-Brock wrote this shortly after the end of World War I, and the chief evidence for his diagnosis he found in the recent history of one great European nation; but, as you will note, he did not make the naive mistake of representing the pooled sense of superiority as a disease peculiar to Germans. He saw in it a generic—though he faintly hoped it might be a curable—disorder of human nature; and he predicted that "we shall have another world war unless we discover and prevent the causes of war in our own minds." His prediction came true in less than two decades—and this second war's duration and vast extent were due not solely to the persistence of the same cause in the minds of Germans, whose self-esteem had been wounded and inflamed by their previous defeat; for another highly gifted people, on another continent, entered the conflict, animated largely by an even more extravagant sense of superiority and a not less exorbitant demand for its recognition by others. In both cases, the outcome showed how exceedingly unfavorable a variation, in the biologist's sense, may be this propensity which the species man has developed in the course of its evolution. For the pooled sense of superiority, even more than the individual variety, is likely to be a fertile breeder of illusory estimates of one's own powers and of a dangerous belittling of those of others.

There were, then, I think, some sound and important insights in Clutton-Brock's diagnosis of the underlying factor

[13] In *op. cit., The Atlantic Monthly,* 1921.

in the particular pathological phenomena—the first two world wars—which he was seeking to understand. And in insisting that the problem was fundamentally a psychological one he was certainly right. But there were also some oversights and some exaggerations in his analysis. In the first place, he seemed to imply that "pooled self-esteem" always makes for overt conflicts—wars, hot or cold. It assuredly makes for group-rivalries; and rivalries often pass over (in the case of groups more frequently than of individuals) into mutual animosities, which in turn tend in time to eventuate in overt conflicts. But they do so only under a certain condition, namely, a belief in the probability of success. And, in spite of the illusion-breeding potency of pooled self-esteem, such a belief does not arise in the case of small and weak nations. They may, in desperation, resist when attacked, but they do not start wars against more powerful neighbors, even when convinced of their own cultural, political, or moral superiority. It is only what are called Great Powers that now are at all likely to initiate great wars. In 1914 there were at least five such powers; there are now only two, the Soviet Union and the United States, though both of these have formed coalitions—more or less solid and dependable—of other nations, which together embrace the greater part of the population of the planet. The principal motive for adherence to these coalitions on one, perhaps on both sides, is *not* national self-esteem, but fear. It is not, however, simply fear of the destruction that in the atomic age would result from another great war, immeasurable though that would be. If that were the sole motive, the fear could obviously be dispelled simply by a determination on the part of all nations which desire to live in peace to submit to any demands which a preponderant Great Power might make; there would be no coalition to *resist* aggression, and all other nations would passively accept the unrestricted domination of one. There are some persons, e.g., Lord Russell, who appear willing to accept this as the only means by which the destruction of most of the human race can now be averted; but they are probably not numerous. In most men, of whatever nationality, there is a vigorous psychological resistance to such submission. In this, one element, unquestionably, is usually a form of both individual and pooled self-esteem—not, here, in the sense of a feeling of superiority but of self-respect, an intense aversion from thinking of themselves and their countrymen as abject cowards. But more powerful, probably, than this, is a deep emotional attachment to their own "way of life"—to their customs, their cultures, their faiths, their pieties (not simply in the religious sense), their traditions—and, above all, their freedom to decide these matters for themselves. It is the fear of losing these that mainly motivates the readiness of many men and nations to join with others (whose customs and pieties may be in many respects different from their own) to resist together any Great Power or Coalition threatening to dominate them all and by force to impose *its* ideology and its way of life upon all of them alike. The personal motivations of the leaders of the governments seeking world-domination I shall not attempt to analyze; what is obvious is that their ambitious designs could not even have been launched unless their subjects had been motivated by pooled self-esteem.

One final comment on Clutton-Brock's essay. He seems to
have believed, or at least hoped, that human nature could
be purged of this desire or propensity, both in its individual and its pooled forms; and it was in the general elimination of it from our minds that he saw the remedy—the necessary and only possible remedy—for the disorders and
the unhappiness which it seemed to him inevitably to generate. In his own words:

> The remedy is a society in which faculties will be no
> longer suppressed, [and] in which men will cure them-
> selves of their self-esteem, not by pooling it, but by caring
> for something not themselves more than for themselves.
> . . . Suppression, good manners, discipline, will never rid
> us of [it]; still it will find a vent in some collective,
> and more dangerous, form, unless we can . . . sublimate
> it into a passion for something not ourselves.

But this prescription was regrettably obscure. It seemed to
contain two ingredients. One of them apparently was a social
order—including a system of economic production—in
which "men are no longer thwarted in the exercise of their
highest faculties." "So long as the mass of men are set by division of labor to tasks in which they cannot satisfy the
higher demands of the self, any demagogue may tempt them
to destroy all that you value. Until they also enjoy and so
value it, it is not secure for you and the world." The other
ingredient seems to be complete disinterestedness and self-
forgetfulness, the exclusion from consciousnes, and thereby
from human motivation, of any reference to the self and of

any desire for values, whether terminal or adjectival, which involve such reference.

But the first of these components of Clutton-Brock's "remedy" could not possibly be realized if economic goods are to be produced in the volume and diversity now demanded by our vast modern civilized societies. Machine-production, with the "division of labor" indispensable for it, is the first prerequisite for the existence of such societies.

The other component of Clutton-Brock's "remedy" seems to call for a more radical transformation of human nature than we have any reason to expect in any foreseeable future —namely, the extirpation of all the motives arising from self-esteem (individual or "pooled") and from emulation, as well as the individual's desire for such terminal values as material goods and normal pleasurable experiences for himself. If there is any truth in what has been said in the present lecture, susceptibility to these desires and motives is inherent in the very constitution of man as a self-conscious animal. The proposal to extirpate these elements and motives in man's constitution is somewhat analogous to a proposal, in physical therapeutics, of total excision of the heart or the liver. Both these organs are subject to, their presence in the body makes possible, the occurrence of certain grave and sometimes fatal disorders. But since their normal functioning is indispensable for the survival of the patient, physicians and surgeons, while now able to prevent or correct some of the disorders, do not recommend the elimination of those organs. Similarly, self-consciousness cannot be eliminated from man's psychical constitution—so long as he remains human; nor is it probable that the affective components made possible by and associated with this—i.e., approbativeness and the desire for at least some degree of self-esteem and the aversion from its opposite, and the propensity to emulation—can be eliminated. They too, as we know, make possible the occurrence of grave disorders of feeling and behavior. If it were at all feasible to eliminate the underlying affective and appetitive components, and if in doing so we should not at the same time be eliminating the psychic sources of much that is generally regarded as most valuable in human experience and behavior, then the radical program of complete extirpation of those components would be the right program. But such extirpation is not feasible, and, if it were, would destroy the springs of action in man which differentiate him from the creatures below him in the scale of being, give rise to his most admirable achievements, and are the conditions of the possibility of civilized social life. Some reasons for so describing them we shall find suggested in the next two lectures by some of the seventeenth- and eighteenth-century writers whose reflections on human nature we shall there review. The "remedy," in short, is to find ways of correcting the worst of the psychic diseases which arise from, and are made possible but not permanently inevitable by, the same constituents of man's make-up by which his happier and distinctively human functioning is made possible; it is not to demand that he shall cease to be human. The needed therapy will doubtless be a long and slow process; we can only hope that the diseases will not destroy the patient before the treatment can be applied.

Lecture IV ❧ ❧ ❧

APPROBATIVENESS AS THE UNIVERSAL, DISTINCTIVE, AND DOMINANT PASSION OF MAN

We shall henceforth be concerned wholly with the reflections of writers in the seventeenth and eighteenth centuries on certain "passions" which they believed to be peculiarly characteristic of man and especially potent in the motivation of his outward behavior—those which I have in the preceding lecture called (a) "approbativeness," the desire for approval or admiration of oneself, one's acts, and one's achievements on the part of one's fellows, and for the expression by them of this feeling—"the love of praise"; (b) "self-esteem," the propensity to or desire for a "good opinion" of oneself and one's qualities, acts, and achievements; and (c) "emulation," the craving for a belief in one's own superiority to others in one or another or all of these respects, and a desire for the recognition of this superiority by those with whom one associates, and for the express admission of it by them. On all these desires or "passions" writers of the period wrote many thousands of pages. But, unfortunately, they had not heard or read the preceding lecture, and they had no really authoritative dictionary "on historical principles" (like the N.E.D.) defining psychological terms. Their terminology, when they discoursed on these subjects, was exceedingly variable and confused. Different names were given, by different writers, to the same "passion" (as shown by the contexts), and the same

129

names to different passions; some of the words have become obsolete, others had connotations unfamiliar to most twentieth-century readers. It seems necessary, therefore, to prefix to the story of this phase of the history of men's ideas about human nature a brief lexicographical preamble.

One important difference between the senses of identical terms in their earlier and contemporary use is that in the former period the same word was often employed to designate both the desire for some object or state-of-things and the object of the desire. For example, the author of an admirable study of Robert Greville's *The Nature of Truth* (1640) has noted that in that work "Fame" and "Honour" are "used frequently for the *desire* for reputation as well as for the honor itself." The same is true of many other seventeenth-century writings; e.g., in Milton's *Lycidas*, "Fame is the spur," etc.—not the achievement of fame but the desire to achieve it, which in the case of the young poet of whom Milton was writing was frustrated by his untimely death. The word "fame" moreover, as many passages could be cited to show, as often, probably more often, referred to contemporary rather than posthumous celebrity, reputation, or renown.

The term "approbativeness," which I shall hereafter use for the desire for the esteem, admiration, and applause of others was, I believe, unknown in the period under consideration, but it can usually be seen from the context that it is this desire that is referred to in such expressions as the "love of fame," the "passion of glory," the "quest of honor," and various other frequently recurring phrases. The noun "pride," which most naturally refers to self-esteem, was also frequently employed to designate approbativeness, the desire for some form or degree of the approbation of others. Since, in the usage of the period, the word was equivocal I shall hereafter sometimes employ it to cover both these senses, especially when quoting texts or titles of books pertinent to one or the other of these "passions."

I shall now quote a number of passages dilating simply upon the universality of "pride" (usually in the sense of the desire for admiration or "glory") among mankind, its irrepressibility, and its primacy as the most powerful of human motives. The collection of examples to be cited will by no means be exhaustive, but sufficient, I think, to indicate the wide—the almost, but not quite, universal— adoption by seventeenth- and eighteenth-century explorers of human nature, of this conception of approbativeness as the most powerful and persistent motive of men's outwardly observable behavior. This way of thinking about man was not a specialty of any one class of writers or any one school of doctrine; the authors of the citations to follow in the present lecture had very little else in common: theologians of different sects, philosophers of conflicting schools, *pensée*-writers and satirists, Catholics, Protestants, and free thinkers. Disagreeing with one another about almost everything else, the authors were of one mind about this.

The Jesuit Mariana wrote in his *De rege* (1599), a famous book in its day:

There is no man, however cultivated or however rustic or rude, who does not burn with an almost infinite *gloriae cupiditas*. . . . No art can extirpate it, no law or fear of punishment repress it. . . . There is no race, no condition,

no age, that is not inflamed with this desire. It is wonderful how much children and even infants are susceptible to
the influence of praise.

Pascal, the most powerful Catholic assailant of the ethics
of the Jesuits, devoted several of his *Pensées* to the same
theme:

> The quest of glory (*la recherche de la gloire*) is the qual-
> ity that is most ineffaceable from the heart of man. . . .
> However much of health and of essential comforts he may
> have, he is not satisfied unless he have a place in men's
> esteem. . . . The sweetness (*douceur*) of glory is so great
> that we love any object to which it is attached, even
> death.[1]

And again:

> Vanity is so anchored in man's heart that a soldier, a
> camp-follower, a cook, a porter, boast and wish to have
> admirers; and the philosophers wish the same; and those
> who write against the desire of glory, glory in having
> written well; and those who read it, desire to have glory
> for having read it; and I who write this have perhaps
> the same desire; and also those who will read what I
> write.[2]

It is "pride" which most of all exemplifies men's *unconsciousness* of the control of their action by nonrational
desires, Malebranche (and many others) observed; it is at
once the most pervasive and the least recognized of motives.

[1] *Pensées*, ed. Giraud, No. 404, No. 153.

[2] *Pensées*, ed. Giraud, No. 150. It will be noted that in
Pascal's terminology, "vanity" and the desire for "glory" (i.e.,
approbativeness in any of its forms or degrees) are synonymous.

Men are not sensible of the heat that is in their hearts, though it gives life and movement to all other parts of their bodies. . . . So is it with vanity: it is so natural to man that he is not sensible of it; and though it is this that gives, so to say, life and movement to most of his thoughts and designs, it often does so in a manner which to him is imperceptible. . . . Men do not sufficiently perceive that it is vanity which gives the impetus to most of their actions.[3]

The Protestant divine, Jacques Abbadie, in his *L'Art de se connoistre soy-même* (*The Art of Knowing Oneself*), explicitly using "pride" in the sense of approbativeness, concludes

that pride . . . is present almost equally in all men. In some it is more manifest, in others less. Not all think as much about being esteemed as others, because there are many whose poverty gives them more pressing preoccupations; but I do not know if one may not say that they all have the propensity for esteem, that the inclination . . . is the same in every man—or rather, that there is only the difference which is due to [divine] grace.

And Abbadie recalls that "Cicero remarks that of all those who have written books on the contempt of fame, none have neglected to affix their names to their works."[4]

Another Huguenot theologian, Jacques La Placette, whose work, like Abbadie's, was translated into English, in his *Treatise on Pride* (*Traité de l'orgueil*, 1693), used the

[3] *Recherche de la verité*, Bk. II, Pt. II, ch. 7 (1674).
[4] *Op. cit.* (1692), p. 433.

term in more than one sense, but it is obviously approbativeness that he has in mind when he observes that

> [Pride] is almost the first emotion which is to be ob-
> served in children, and as soon as they can talk they give
> evidence that they love to be caressed, flattered and ap-
> plauded. On the other hand, the dying are not exempt
> from it, witness the orders which the most part of them
> give about their funerals. . . . In a word, one may say
> that pride begins life and ends it.

Pride, however, as we have seen, is used by many writers
of the period to designate both the fear of disapprobation
and the desire for admiration and applause. Both, of course,
are forms of what I am calling approbativeness, but some of
these writers dwell chiefly upon the negative aspect of this
motive and some upon its positive aspect, the desire for
reputation, admiration, and applause. The former tendency
is illustrated by the following passage from John Locke.
The author of the *Essay Concerning Human Understanding*
was sure that "there is a divine law which God has set to the
actions of men, whether promulgated to them by the light of
nature or the voice of revelation," but he was equally sure
that this law, as such, seldom, if ever, influences men's conduct.

> Virtue and vice are names pretended, and supposed
> everywhere to stand for actions in their own nature right
> and wrong. . . . But yet, whatever is pretended, this is
> visible, that these names, virtue and vice, in the particular
> instances of their application through the several nations
> and societies of men in the world are constantly attrib-
> uted only to such actions as are in each society in

reputation or discredit. . . . Thus, the measure of what is everywhere called and esteemed virtue and vice is, the approbation or dislike, praise or blame, which, by a secret or tacit consent, establishes itself in the several societies, tribes and clubs of men in the world.

And it is the universal *desire* for approbation and the aversion from blame that motivate men's conformity to the locally accepted standard:

He who imagines commendation and disgrace not to be strong motives to men, to accommodate themselves to the opinions and rules of those with whom they converse, seems little skilled in the nature or history of mankind: the greatest part whereof he shall find to govern themselves chiefly, if not solely, by this law of fashion; and so they do that which keeps them in reputation with their company, little regarding the laws of God or the magistrate. . . . He must be of a strange and unusual constitution, who can content himself to live in constant disgrace and disrepute with his own particular society. . . . This is a burden too great for human sufferance; and he must be made up of irreconcilable contradictions, who can take pleasure in company, and yet be insensible of contempt and disgrace from his companions.[5]

Locke, it will be noted, though he recognizes both the positive and negative aspects of approbativeness, seems to have considered the latter—aversion from disapprobation—the more prevalent and potent motive. He seems also to have overlooked or, when writing on this topic, to have forgotten the fact that there are different degrees of approbation, and therefore of approbativeness, and he conse-

[5] *Op. cit.*, Bk. II, ch. 28, sections 10-12.

quently left emulativeness, "ambition," the "love of glory," out of account altogether. In this he differs from most of his seventeenth-century predecessors and eighteenth-century successors, who, as the passages cited from them show, tended to dwell exclusively upon these latter motives. There has been, in fact, a curious one-sidedness in the majority of the analysts of human motives, both in the earlier period and in our own century. Those who were keenly aware of the potency of the "love of praise" were rarely equally sensible of the potency of the fear of blame, and *vice versa*. This is, I think, a general fact in the history of ideas concerning the motivations of human conduct which it is important for the explorer of that history to bear in mind. For one of its consequences has been a neglect of the problems, mentioned in Lecture III, of the comparative potency and the relative frequency of these two springs of—or deterrents from—action. This, of course, is a question to which no strictly verifiable answer can be given; it is a quantitative and statistical question, and we have no statistical evidence on it. But it is not on that account a meaningless or inconsequential question. And most of us, I suspect, when asked, would be ready with an answer to it, based upon our own introspection and our observations and conjectural explanations of the behavior of other people. In the seventeenth and eighteenth centuries the question was, so far as I can recall, never discussed or even definitely formulated; and those who expatiated upon the nature of man's dominant and universal passion mostly found it—not, as Locke did, in the fear of "disgrace and disrepute"—but in the craving for reputation, praise, and applause.

For example, in the mid-eighteenth century, Dr. Johnson saw in human behavior almost exclusively the types of motivation which Locke had neglected. He wrote in *The Rambler* (1751):

Distinction is so pleasing to the pride of man that a great part of the pain and pleasure of life arise from the gratification or disappointment of an incessant wish for superiority. . . . Proportionate to the prevalence of the love of praise is the variety of means by which its attainment is attempted. Every man, however hopeless his pretensions may appear, has some project by which he hopes to rise to reputation; some art by which he imagines that the attention of the world will be attracted; some quality, good or bad, which discriminates him from the common herd of mortals, and by which others may be persuaded to love, or compelled to fear him.[6]

(Here, it will be observed, there is a confusion of four distinct motives, but the chief emphasis is upon emulative approbativeness.) No one went further than Johnson in asserting the constant pressure of this passion: "Scarce any man," he declared in *The Adventurer*, "is abstracted for one moment from his vanity." I regret to add that he made no exception of the academic profession; he thought the most unpleasing consequences of this human trait especially conspicuous among scholars in universities, and said so in a beautifully typical piece of Johnsonese:

Discord, who found means to roll her apples into the banquetting chamber of the goddesses, has had the ad-

[6] *Rambler*, No. 164.

dress to scatter her laurels in the seminaries of learning. The friendship of students and of beauties is for the most part equally sincere and equally durable; as both depend for happiness on the regard of others, on that of which the value arises merely from comparison, they are both exposed to perpetual jealousies, and both incessantly employed in schemes to intercept the praises of each other.[7]

Yet Johnson felt constrained to admit that this motive, though it causes rivalries and animosities, is also useful, since it "incites competition" and "initiates a contagion of diligence."

These remarks of Dr. Johnson's in his essays of the 1750's have been introduced out of their chronological place in this selection of texts because, in their contrast with Locke's, they serve especially well to illustrate the tendency of writers on the subject to dwell upon only one side of the shield—not upon both the positive and negative forms of approbativeness. But the most celebrated, and a much more lengthy, English disquisition on "pride" had appeared nearly a quarter-century earlier—Edward Young's poem *Love of Fame the Universal Passion* (1726-8).[8] Young, an Anglican divine of high social and ecclesiastical position (he was chaplain to George II), unmistakably showed in his poem that he was himself no exception to the generalization expressed in the title.

The *Love of Praise*, howe'er conceal'd by art,

[7] *The Adventurer*, No. 45 (1753).

[8] Form of the title in the 1792 (posthumous) edition of his *Works*, "revised and corrected by himself."

Reigns, more or less, and glows in ev'ry heart:
The *proud*, to gain it, toils on toils endure;
The *modest* shun it but to make it sure.
O'er globes and sceptres, now on thrones it swells;
Now trims the midnight lamp in college cells . . .
It aids the *dancer's* heel, the *writer's* head,
And heaps the plain with mountains of the dead;
Nor ends with *life;* but nods in sable *plumes,*
Adorns our *herse,* and flatters on our *tombs.*[9]

So, in a series of what he calls "characteristical satires,"
Young traces to this common source the activities, and the
follies, of all classes and types of men; the scholar parad-
ing his erudition—

Some for *renown* on scraps of learning dote,
And think they grow immortal as they *quote;*

the philosopher, the soldier, the politician, the outwardly
devout—

Some go to Church, *proud* humbly to repent,
And come back much more guilty than they went.
One way they *look,* another way they *steer,*
Pray to the *Gods;* but would have mortals hear;

the *nouveau riche,* and equally

Those that on glorious ancestors enlarge,
Produce their *debt,* instead of their *discharge;*

the art collector, the sporting squire, the social climber, the
literary critic—a class who

[9] *Op. cit.,* 2nd. ed., 1728, Satire I, p. 7, italics are the poet's.

All will judge, and with one single aim,
To gain themselves, and not the writer, fame.

Two of the satires are devoted to exhibiting the special forms which this craving takes in women. And the poet—in this still adhering to a convention—does not fail to admit that it is the same universal passion that engenders his own effusions, that his satire is a kind of boomerang:

O thou, myself! . . .
Thou, too, art wounded with the common dart,
And Love of Fame lies throbbing at thy heart.[10]

The admission was even more pointedly made by a lesser poet, Cuthbert Shaw (1766):

Ev'n now, whilst I incline
To paint the vot'ries kneeling at thy shrine,
Whilst others' follies freely I impart,
Thy power resistless flutters round my heart,
Prompts me this common weakness to disclose,
(Myself the very coxcomb I expose).[11]

But Young's reflections on the love of fame take quite another turn before his poem ends; this we shall see in a later lecture.

[10] *Op. cit.*, Satire II, p. 40.

[11] *The Poems of Cuthbert Shaw and Thomas Russell*, ed. by Eric Partridge (1925), p. 76. I may add that none of the eighteenth-century confessions of this sort equal in grimly ironic hyperbole some (I believe) unpublished lines by a contemporary poet-scholar which he permits me to quote:

I am hungry for praise:
I would to God it were not so—

As some of the passages already cited illustrate, it was not merely upon the fairly obvious fact of the universality of this craving that these and other writers liked to dwell; many of them sought to find in it the common root of nearly all the seemingly diverse emotions and appetencies of men. It became, then, one of the favorite pursuits of analysts of human nature to reduce most of the other "passions" to one or another of the forms of "pride," to show it to be the true explanation of actions which those who performed them supposed to spring from quite other motives, to trace its workings in the most various situations of social life, and to exhibit it as the force which keeps every vocation going, except those which serve the primary physical needs of food and shelter. Theses of this sort were obviously difficult to prove, unless by an appeal to the introspection of readers, which, if the theses were true, was not likely to be an altogether candid or competent witness. An analysis of the inconsistencies between men's behavior and their professed reasons for it could, however, provide a good deal of plausible evidence for such theses; so far as they had a logical status, they were essentially hypotheses advanced as explaining the observable facts of behavior better than any alternative assumptions about motivation. But the writers of *pensées,* maxims, apothegms, often just threw them out

---

> That I must live through all my days
> Yearning for what I'll never know.
> I even hope that when I'm dead
> The worms won't find me wholly vicious,
> But as they masticate my head
> Will smack their lips and cry 'delicious!'

as so manifestly true that any fairly shrewd and realistic-minded reader must recognize their truth without requiring argument.

Most of the examples of this which might be cited are also apposite to another part of the general subject, with which I wish to deal separately later—the evaluations of "pride"—and I shall therefore present here only a few illustrations of this tendency.

As extreme an example as any is provided by the great Lord Halifax,[12] who sought to find in pride the principal source of most men's love for their sweethearts and wives and even their children. In his *Advice to a Daughter*, about 1680, he writes:

> Most Men are . . . so far *Philosophers*, as to allow, that the greatest part of pleasure lieth in the *Mind;* and in pursuance of that *Maxim*, there are few who do not place the Felicity more in the Opinion of the World, of their being *prosperous Lovers*, than in the *Blessing* it self, how much soever they appear to value it.

And among his "Miscellaneous Thoughts" Halifax sets down that:

> The Desire of having Children is as much the Effect of Vanity as of Good-nature. Men love their Children, not because they are promising plants, but because they are theirs. . . . Pride in this, as in many other things, is often mistaken for love.

[12] George Savile, Marquis of Halifax (1633-1695) an important figure in the controversies preceding the civil wars, best known as a writer for his pamphlet "Character of a Trimmer," published in 1688.

Fantastically exaggerated, no doubt. But this is a striking
example of the tendency of acute minds in the period to
minimize the part of instinct and natural affection in order
to trace to what they conceived to be man's strongest and
most distinctive passion as many as possible of his propensities. And an example, also, of the way in which this
tendency sometimes led them to see actual but unflattering
facts about men. For, overstated though it obviously is,
Halifax's remark upon the place of egotism in parental
love can hardly be said to be altogether unsupported by
observation of the behavior of some of the seemingly
most philoprogenitive of parents.

While Halifax thus sought in "pride" the root of parental
affection, a psychologist of the same period found in the
desire for praise the principal motivation of the most
famous example in classical history of the sacrifice of
parental affection upon the altar of patriotism. "The *fermete
barbare* which Brutus manifested in causing his own sons
to be executed before his eyes" was not so disinterested
as it seemed; "the most excellent of the Latin poets discovers its motives in these words: *Vincet amor patriae,
laudumque immensa cupido.*"[13] This caustic comment
might have implied merely that Brutus was unaware of his
true motive; but there were other seventeenth-century analysts of human nature who opined that men *are* always
conscious that the *laudum cupido* prompts all their actions,
but that they always try to conceal the fact. La Bruyère
wrote:

[13] Abbadie, *L'art de se connoistre soy-même*, p. 285. The line
quoted is from Vergil, *Aeneid* VI, 283.

At heart men wish to be esteemed, and they carefully conceal this wish because they wish to pass for virtuous, and
because to desire to gain from virtue any advantage
beyond itself would not be to be virtuous but to love
esteem and praise—in other words, to be vain. Men are
very vain, and they hate nothing so much as being regarded as vain.[14]

The ideas concerning human nature which we have just
been recalling were frequently combined with another thesis,
though they did not strictly imply it: namely, that "pride"
—probably in both of its senses, but certainly in that of
approbativeness—is not only a passion universally prevalent among men but is also *peculiar* to the *genus homo,* the
psychic differentia of man on his emotive and appetitive (as distinct from his intellectual and cognitive) side. It
was, perhaps, at least conceivable that some of the higher
animals (about whose subjective life we *know* virtually
nothing) experience transitory emotions similar to self-
esteem, on the successful accomplishment of some biological
urge, or, in the case of certain domesticated and trained
animals, of some trick taught them by their masters. But it
could hardly be supposed that they are dominated, as men
are, by a besetting desire for the belief that a certain kind
of *thought* about them as individuals—an approving judgment and a feeling of admiration—exists on the part of
other individuals of their own species. It is by virtue of this
latter "passion," then, that man is inwardly differentiated
from all the other creatures below him in the Scale of Being,

[14] *Les Charactères: De l'homme* (1696), 1, 24.

and it is in it that the investigator of man's inner nature must seek the primary cause, and therefore the explanation, of the myriad modes of outward behavior observable only in him.

This being assumed, it obviously followed that all of man's "passions," his "springs of action," fall into two classes. That he is of a dual constitution had, of course, long been a commonplace; but the traditional dualism had been that of the senses and the reason, or the "flesh" and the "spirit." But in view of the foregoing considerations, it appeared that the fundamental dichotomy, the one pertinent to the understanding of his distinctive ways of acting, is that between all the kinds of desires common to him and other animals and the specifically human appetite—in short, "pride" in the sense of approbativeness.

Since this feature of the thought of the period has not, I believe, usually been noted by historians of psychology and philosophy, some examples of it must be here adduced.[15] Mariana in his *De rege* wrote that

> since the desire of pleasure is common to us and the animals and is chiefly defined in corporeal terms, virtue has the rather been made to consist in the arduous and men are excited to the pursuit of virtue by the desire of glory.

Hobbes did not think the effects of the "passion of glory"— which for him usually meant emulative self-esteem—bene-

[15] We have already encountered one example of it in the first citation from Lord Halifax, above, p. 142.

ficial; but he too defined it as the distinctively "mental" and specifically human appetite.

> Whatsoever seems good, is pleasant, and relates either to the senses or the mind. But all the *mind's* pleasure is either glory, (or to have a good opinion of oneself), or relates to glory in the end; the rest are sensual, or conducing to sensuality, which may be all comprehended under the word *conveniences.*[16]

La Placette subsumes all man's numerous desires under two classes: *la volupté,* which is not peculiar to man, and the love of glory, praise, and the like, which is; and he somewhat hastily concludes that the motives of man's activities—or at least of his "sins"—are about equally divided between the two.[17] Abbadie in *L'Art de se connoistre soy-même* dwells upon the fortunate contrariety of *la volupté* and *l'orgueil:* "Pride and the love of pleasure are two passions which, though they come from the same source, which is *l'amour-propre,* nevertheless have in them always some mutual opposition. The love of pleasure lowers us, pride seeks to raise us higher."[18]

This dichotomy of human motives was adopted, though not constantly or consistently, by Rousseau; "it is easy to see," he writes, "that all our labors are directed upon two objects only, namely, the commodities of life for oneself, and consideration on the part of others." "Consideration" in both French and English usage in the eighteenth century,

[16] *Leviathan*, ch. 13, 2; italics mine.
[17] *Traité de l'Orgueil*, pp. 114-115.
[18] *Op. cit.*, p. 347.

it should be remembered, usually meant, not kindness or thoughtfulness, but "being highly or favorably considered," i.e., esteem, admiration, or deference. It is one of Rousseau's numerous synonyms for the object of the passion of "pride"; another is "opinion," which, as he employs it, signifies usually the good opinion of others. And the other terms which he uses as interchangeable with *l'orgueil*, as well as his reasonings about that passion, make it evident that he has commonly in mind emulative approbativeness; among his names for it are *la fureur de se distinguer, l'ardeur de faire parler de soi, le désir universel de réputation, d'honneurs et de préférences, l'amour propre.* This last term is expressly distinguished by him from *l'amour de soi.* It is the latter, self-love, which is, in Rousseau's psychology, the basic and universal passion, "the origin and principle" (I am quoting from *Émile*) "of all the others, the only one which is born with a man and never leaves him as long as he lives, . . . a passion primitive, innate, anterior to any other, and of which all the others are in a sense merely modifications."[19]

But these derivatives of man's fundamental *amour de soi* (which is "always good and always in conformity with the order of things") fall into the two classes already indicated. In the one class, we "are concerned only with ourselves," i.e., are not thinking of other persons at all, but only seeking to satisfy those desires and impulses which arise in us spontaneously and "naturally," without any conscious contrast between the self and others. These are not peculiar to our

[19] *Oeuvres*, 1865 ed., II, p. 183.

species. But the second class, summed up under the name *l'amour-propre,* always involve comparison, *se comparer aux autres,* and thus manifest themselves in emulativeness and in activities inspired thereby. And, as will more clearly appear later, in connection with another aspect of Rousseau's thought, it is really emulation that is the *distinctive* thing in man, arising in him as soon as intelligence arises. Unhappily for the neatness of this schematism, Rousseau's views compel him to regard this passion *both* as a form or subspecies of self-love and as its very antithesis. Somehow or other, *l'amour de soi* gets transformed by *des causes étrangères* into desires which "reverse its primary object."

Another reason was sometimes propounded for regarding the emulative form of pride as that which chiefly differentiates man from the animals. It was apparently already a commonplace that the obvious external contrast between them is that an animal species remains, in its nature and behavior, the same throughout time, whereas man's mode of life, his activities, and his products exhibit a cumulative change. Some explanation of this manifest difference was needed; it was sometimes found in man's craving for distinction, which, perpetually urging the individual to surpass the attainments and performances of others, becomes the cause of the progress of the race. So Burke wrote in 1756:

Although imitation is one of the great instruments used by Providence in bringing our nature towards its perfection, yet if men gave themselves up to imitation entirely, and each followed the other, and so on in an eternal circle, it is easy to see that there never could be any improvement amongst them. Men must remain as brutes do, the same at the end that they are at this day, and that they were in the beginning of the world. To prevent this, God has planted in man a sense of ambition, and a satisfaction arising from the contemplation of his excelling his fellows in something deemed valuable amongst them. It is this passion that drives men to all the ways we see in use of signalising themselves, and that tends to make whatever excites in a man the idea of this distinction so very pleasant.[20]

Both these conceptions of the differentia of man, "pride" and progressiveness, are combined by Rousseau when, in the *Second Discourse*, he offers one of the first modern attempts to trace the gradual stages of man's psychological development from his original animal condition to the state of civilization. The animals are free from "pride," and so was primitive man,[21] for primitive man was simply an animal, a variety of the orang-outangs, living as they do. He was, however, an exceptionally clever orang-outang; there was latent in him the germ of a greater intelligence which, in the course of ages, enabled him to invent simple tools and to develop language. But upon this initial, purely intellectual, differentiation of his kind, there soon supervened an affective one; man began to compare himself first of all with the other animals and to feel a gratifying sense of superiority to them. He became, in short, for the first time, self-

[20] *Essay on the Sublime and Beautiful*, Pt. I, p. 17.

[21] Rousseau very likely got the suggestion of this from Pope: in the State of Nature

    Pride then was not, nor arts that pride to aid;

    Man walk'd with beast, joint tenant of the shade.

Essay on Man, III, 151-2.

conscious; and simultaneously with self-consciousness pride
was born:

> Le premier regard qu'il porta sur lui-même y produisit
> le premier mouvement d'orgueil; c'est ainsi que, sachant
> à peine à distinguer les rangs, et se contemplant par son
> espèce, il se préparait de loin à y prétendre par son
> individu;

i.e., comparative self-esteem, once introduced into the
human mind in the form of pride of race, was easily transformed into the habit of comparing oneself with other individuals of one's own species and of feeling oneself, or
liking to think of oneself, as superior to *them*. This was, at
first, *mere* self-esteem, a pleasing sense of actual superiority.
How it passed over into invidious and, indeed, pugnacious
approbativeness, Rousseau hardly makes clear; he is apparently unaware, or only dimly aware, of the difference between them. At all events, he somewhat abruptly substitutes
the one for the other.

Man's other specific differentia—Rousseau himself calls
it that—namely, *la faculté de se perfectionner*, or perfectibility, is closely related in his thought to the conception of
"pride." For though man's so-called progress is made
possible by his possession of superior intelligence, the
motive which actuates his exercise of this faculty is, for
Rousseau as later for Burke, the individual's insatiable need
to feel himself, and to show himself, and to be recognized as,
superior to others. From this come all of civilized man's
achievements—his sciences, his arts, his institutions—and
all his miseries and most of his vices. Man's pride, in short,

is the cause of his so-called perfectibility. Pondering on the almost unlimited potency of this passion, Rousseau is moved to ejaculate: *O fureur de se distinguer, que ne pouvez-vous point!* He is here perhaps consciously echoing Vergil's *quid non mortalia pectora cosis;* but for "greed of gold" he significantly substitutes "the craving for distinction."

This ejaculation over the unlimited potency of the *fureur de se distinguer* is not to be understood as an eulogy of that passion. Rousseau is not saying that it begot one class of good things, *viz.* the sciences and arts, and also certain bad things, men's follies and miseries; he is saying that the craving for distinction is a manifestation of man's folly and the principal source of his miseries. An exposition of the arguments by which he seeks to prove this will be more pertinent to the theme of a later lecture.

Lecture V ✻ ✻ ✻

THE "LOVE OF PRAISE" AS THE INDISPENSABLE SUBSTITUTE FOR "REASON AND VIRTUE" IN SEVENTEENTH- AND EIGHTEENTH-CENTURY THEORIES OF HUMAN NATURE

It is apparent from what has already been said that the recognition of "pride" as the distinctive and ubiquitous peculiarity of man did not necessarily carry with it, in this age, the implication that man is fortunate in possessing it. Even though "pride" was admitted to be a nonsensual appetency, and one which sharply differentiates man from the animals, man might conceivably be all the worse for having this additional and anomalous passion. On this issue of the appraisal of "pride" two opposed currents of doctrine run through the seventeenth and eighteenth centuries. The appraisal depended partly upon the sense attached to the term "pride" and partly upon the religious preconceptions of the appraiser. Christianity had inherited, chiefly from later Judaism, especially from the Wisdom Literature,[1] an intense ethical inwardness, a preoccupation with the nature of the feelings or motives from which an act springs more than with the value of its consequences; some emotions and springs of action were supposed to be known intuitively, or through revelation, to be morally wrong, irrespective of their outward effects. "Keep thy *heart* with all diligence, for out of *it* are the issues of life" (Proverbs,

[1] On this see Lovejoy, "The Origins of Ethical Inwardness in Jewish Thought," *American Journal of Theology*, XI (1907), pp. 228-249.

4:3). "Look in and not out," may be said to have been the first rule of life for the earnest believer. There resulted that extreme and painful introversion, that daily and sometimes almost hourly practice of self-examination, of suspiciously and apprehensively probing one's inward parts, which was so characteristic a feature of religious experience in these centuries. For our own more extroverted generation it is difficult to enter with imaginative sympathy into this large area of the life of our more religious forebears; to us this species of spiritual hypochrondria, this habit of constantly feeling one's moral pulse, seems a morbid and repellent thing. But that is another story. What is pertinent here is that "pride" in the sense of self-esteem, individual or racial was admittedly a sin—indeed, according to many theologians, the worst of the deadly sins—and humility the most necessary of the virtues. There could, then, be no possibility, for devout minds, of a favorable appraisal of *this* inner state, either as an emotion or as a spring of action. The awkward aspect of this situation—to digress a moment from my immediate theme—was that the more honest and more subtle practicers of moral introspection found pride so pervasive of man's consciousness that it *could* not be extirpated, since it can and does feed upon its own opposite. That humility, when, through painful self-discipline, one attains it, becomes thereby a source of self-esteem was an old story. For the "worldly," especially for the satirists either of the religious type of character or of man in general, this has always been a pleasing comic paradox. But to sincere religious minds it was a tragic fact which their own self-searching revealed to them. Thus La Placette, whose *Traité de l'orgueil* is mainly a long exhortation against pride, is finally compelled to admit that "even the children of God, and the most regenerate and the most saintly among them, are not altogether exempt from it."

It is very difficult to see in others faults from which one is oneself free, or to perform any good action, without some secret-applause. Even humility very often begets pride; we applaud ourselves for being humble; and when, after profound meditation, we arrive at the conclusion that we are nothing, either before God or in ourselves, when we look upon ourselves with the last degree of contempt, this contempt seems to us so fine and right, that we find in it a reason to exalt ourselves higher than before; . . . so that this sin rebuilds itself upon its own ruins.

Jacques Esprit goes still further; the outward show of humility not only begets pride (in the sense of a secret self-esteem), but it is itself begotten of pride (in the sense of a desire to think of oneself, and to be regarded by one's fellows, as superior to them) :

Since we find by experience that Pride masters and governs Man, and makes him altogether intractable, we may easily conclude that when he despises and blames himself, his words betray [i.e., play false to] his thoughts; that he makes use of Humility to others, to raise himself above them; and that he would never act so contrary to his haughty and proud Temper did not he conceive that nothing is fitter to make him great than a voluntary Humiliation.[2]

[2] La Placette, *op. cit.*, pp. 99-100; Esprit, *De la fausseté des vertus humaines*, English tr. (1708), p. 174. For Burton on the

This conception, then, of the irrational approbativeness of men as the dynamic of good conduct was one of the favorite themes of social psychology from the sixteenth to the late eighteenth century. The observation that this motive is the next best thing to actual virtue, and serves much the same purpose, was, it should be said, not original with the writers of this period. Cicero had remarked in the *De Finibus:* "The sages, taking nature as their guide, make virtue their aim; on the other hand, men who are not perfect and yet are endowed with superior minds *(ingeniis excellentibus praediti)* are often incited by glory, which has the appearance and likeness of *honestas.*" This recognition of a higher and a lower class of "good" men—the lower being actuated in their behavior by an imperfect motive—had been passed down through the later Middle Ages. Dante in the *Paradiso* assigns the lovers of fame and honor to the sphere of Mercury:

This little star is furnish'd with good spirits
Whose moral lives were busy to that end
That honor and renown might wait on them.

Yet, though "good spirits," these fell short of the love of the true good:

And when desires thus err in their intention,
True love must needs ascend with slacker beam.[3]

---

same theme, see *Anatomy of Melancholy*, Pt. I, Sect. 2, Memb. 3, Subs. 14.

[3] Cicero, *De Finibus*, V, 69; Dante, *Paradiso*, VI, 117-122 (Cary tr.). As Cary notes, Dante is here contrasting the love of

But the theme had, so far as I know, never before been so elaborated and so constantly reiterated as in the seventeenth and eighteenth centuries.

Yet a closely related idea was developed in the thought of the seventeenth- and eighteenth-century writers and was constantly reiterated throughout these centuries. It was a thesis which went beyond those of Cicero and Dante. Both of the latter had asserted that approbativeness, though not precisely a virtue, produced in some men almost the same effect. They did not, however, assert that all men are at all times controlled by this motive. But in the later period which we are examining it came to be a widely accepted premise that all men are incapable of being actuated by any other motive in their social conduct, that the craving for admiration or applause is not only universal in the human species but also that it was ingeniously implanted in man by his Creator as a substitute for the Reason and Virtue which he does not possess, and is the sole subjective prompting of good conduct, and the motive of virtually all the modes of behavior necessary for the good order of society and the progress of mankind.

On the eve of the seventeenth century the Jesuit Mariana launched a vigorous counterattack on the conventional condemnation of this motive. Many men, he observed, denounce the *laudis studium* on the ground that virtue should be loved for its own sake, and place this desire *in rebus turpissimis;* but those who do so "do not sufficiently consider whether,

---

the highest Good, the Beatific Vision, with the desire for fame and honor.

while they strengthen modesty, they do not by this sort of talk weaken the foundations of human life."

Who does not see that it is by the desire for praise that men are powerfully stirred to undertake great deeds? For none—or certainly very few—would ever have braved danger for the defence of the common weal, for their country, or for their own dignity, or would have preferred the public good to their own, or despising the comforts of life, have devoted themselves to the study of wisdom, unless they had been incited by the desire and hope of immortality. Turn over the annals of the past, recall the records of ancient times: you will without doubt find that it is from this source that the bravest commanders, the most prudent legislators, the greatest philosophers have arisen. . . . The *gloriae studium,* therefore, is not the creation of vulgar opinion, but is implanted by Nature, as is shown by the fact that it is in a wonderful way present in all men. . . . Who, therefore, is so inept a judge as to think we should vituperate such a desire, and not rather bestow the highest praises upon it.[4]

This was manifestly (though, no doubt, unconsciously) a total repudiation of the teaching of the Sermon on the Mount, uttered by a zealous member of a Christian religious order.

John Milton in 1637 also dilated upon the potency of the desire for praise as the motive for most of the more valuable activities of men, but gave it a different turn. Familiar as it is, the passage on "fame" in *Lycidas* is worth examining in order to bring out its relations of both similarity and differ-

[4] *De rege,* pp. 235 ff., p. 245.

ence to other ideas on the subject in the same period. By
"fame" Milton clearly means primarily not (what the word
probably usually conveys to the modern reader of the lines)
posthumous, but contemporary, reputation and applause.
About the desire for this he is in agreement with most of his
predecessors and contemporaries; it is a human weakness,
an "infirmity," though the "last," that is, the most inexpugnable, infirmity, "of noble mind." He also shares the
prevalent opinion that it is a beneficial infirmity, needful
to arouse men to overcome the solicitations of pleasure
and "live laborious days"; without it even the poet would
not exert his talents. (There is perhaps a hint of introspection and confession in this.) But the youthful poet who is
the subject of the elegy had been cut off before he could
enjoy the "fair guerdon" which he had craved; and this is
a common experience:

> Comes the blind Fury with the abhorred shears,
> And slits the thin-spun life.—But not the praise!

The reward—the sufficient reward—is still "fame," the
knowledge of the approving judgment of another; but not
the fallible judgment of men. The final court of appeal for
those who seek praise is in

> Those pure eyes
> And perfect witness of all-judging Jove.
> Of so much fame in heaven expect thy mead.

Milton thus identifies approbativeness as an element of the
religious consciousness. The lines suggest that the implicit
object of this universal desire is the attestation of the worth

of one's act or one's achievement by an Ideal Critic, an
Approver whose judgment is incorruptible and whose standard of appraisal is intrinsically valid. It is a conception
of deity significantly different from those most conspicuous
in Milton's later theology, and from that which Christian
thought took over largely from Aristotle, of a transcendent
and self-contained Perfection whom it was man's final end
to "enjoy forever" through contemplation. Whatever be
thought of it as a theology, it clearly corresponds to one of
the most potent functions of the idea of God in religious
experience. But Milton's introduction of it into his poem
may be fairly presumed to be a reflection of the preoccupation of so many of his contemporaries with the evalution of
the "love of fame" as a factor in human feeling and behavior.

Abbadie admits this appetency is a puzzling element in
man's make-up; "it is," he says, "certainly not easy to find
*la première et la plus ancienne raison pour laquelle nous
aymons à être estimés.*" He clearly feels that it is a queer
thing, calling for explanation, that we should care—more,
perhaps, than about anything else—about the good opinion
of others of our species about us, since "this esteem is
something foreign (*étranger*) to ourselves and is placed
outside of us (*éloigné*)." This oddity of man, he goes on,
may at first seem explicable as a consequence of that other
desire which we share with the animals, *la volupté*, the love
of pleasure. But it is no solution of the problem "to say that
we desire the esteem of others because of the pleasure which
attaches to it." It may be true that "we are *sensible* of glory
only through the pleasure that accompanies it"; but the

question is, why *does* pleasure accompany it. It pleases us because we desire it; but what makes us desire it? Is it not, in fact, something "which we desire on its own account"? Nor does it solve the problem any better to explain this passion by its utility to the individual—by what, in a later terminology, would be called its survival-value. For though it sometimes "helps us to succeed in our designs and procures us certain advantages in society," it frequently has the contrary effect; it incites us to arduous labor and leads the soldier into the imminent deadly breach. "What utility can have been envisaged by those heroes who gave their lives to gain honor—a Mutius, Leonidas, Codrus, Curtius?"[5] Nor will Abbadie admit that the craving for the esteem of others is a derivative of self-esteem, that the good opinion of our fellows is valued simply because "it confirms the good opinion we have of ourselves." For the two desires vary independently; and men in general, he thinks, "prefer to have faults that are esteemed than good qualities which society (*le monde*) does not esteem," and like "to gain consideration for qualities which they know very well they do not possess."[6] Nor, again,

> is there any more justification for imagining that we desire esteem because we desire distinction and like to raise ourselves above others. This is to explain the cause by the effect. It is not because we crave distinction that we crave esteem; it is because we crave esteem that we seek to distinguish ourselves by standing out (*sortant*)

[5] *L'Art de se connoistre soy-même*, 1698, pp. 410 ff.
[6] *Ibid.*, p. 413.

from the multitude or from the obscurity in which we were at first.[7]

Our devout psychologist concludes that this inclination is inexplicable as a derivative of any other human trait or as an effect of any known natural cause; it can only be explained teleologically—that is, "the reason for it can be found only in the wisdom of the Creator." It is to be borne in mind that, according to a thesis of Abbadie's mentioned in the first lecture, it is psychologically impossible for the reason, as such, to move the will. All choice must be the effect of a specific emotive susceptibility manifesting itself in a desire. Even the Creator could not bring about what is intrinsically impossible. Having, then, necessarily made man a creature incapable of being "moved to action by reason alone, independently of feeling," but nevertheless wishing him to be capable of *acting* reasonably and living in society, the Deity took the "precaution" to implant in him this nonrational yet needful appetite, to counteract his other and more dangerous craving, *la volupté,* and thus "to lead us to honorable and praiseworthy actions which are so suitable to the dignity of our nature, and at the same time to unite us the better with one another." In short, "it pleased the wisdom of the Creator to give us, for judge of our actions, not only our reason, which allows itself to be corrupted by pleasure, but also the reason of other men, which is not so easily seduced," since "they are not so partial to us as we are to ourselves." (This last observation of Abbadie's is an especially shrewd one.) God, therefore,

[7] *Ibid.*, p. 414.

has placed this *penchant* in us for the good of society; for it is this desire of being esteemed that makes us courteous and considerate, obliging and decent, makes us wish for decorum and gentle manners in social relations. Who, moreover, does not know that it is to this natural desire of glory that we owe the fine arts, the most sublime sciences, the wisest governments, the most just institutions, and in general all that is most admirable in society?[8]

Thus, "the animal world is a society of persons united by feeling (*le sentiment*)." Abbadie is possibly thinking of the instincts of the so-called social animals. "The world of rational beings (*le monde raisonnable*) is a society of persons united by esteem"[9]—that is, by their mutual desire for esteem, respect, or admiration. In sum, "the love of esteem" is "the means of which the Author of Nature made use *pour perfectionner la société*, as the love of pleasure is designed to form it."[10] (The last distinction, as we have already seen, was later to be made much of by Burke and Rousseau.) Abbadie, however, after thus insisting upon the benign function of "pride," which he at first uses as a synonym for the desire for esteem or "glory," then becomes confused in his terminology and treats the latter as only one of the "branches," or subspecies, of "pride," the others being presumption, vanity, ambition, and arrogance. The influence of

[8] *Ibid.*, p. 423.

[9] *Op. cit.*, p. 417. Abbadie, however, somewhat inconsistently with his fundamental psychological principles, adds a third "world," *le monde religieux*, which is "united by natural religion," i.e., by "conscience."

[10] *Ibid.*, pp. 424-5.

the medieval classifications of these, as in the Parson's Tale in Chaucer, is apparent here; and Abbadie proceeds to dilate upon the *dèréglemens*, the pernicious and abnormal aspects of each. This part of his psychologizing belongs, of course, to the other side of the picture.

An English contemporary of Abbadie's, the court physician and religious poet and essayist Sir Richard Blackmore, who took a pompous pleasure in bestowing the plaudits of the author of *Creation* upon the achievements of the Author of creation, dilates on

> the admirable Conduct of Providence, which makes use of culpable Passions and irregular Principles, substituted by Men in the place of sincere Merit, to bring about Ends of the greatest Importance and Benefit to Mankind. . . . But when Principles of Vertue are wanting, as apparently they are in the Mass of Mankind, the Desire of Popularity and False Glory, by the wise Administration of the Moderator of the World, in a great Measure supplies their absence.[11]

The desire of "popularity and false glory," however, obviously had a negative counterpart which worked to the same end—the fear of the bad opinion of others, of "dishonor" in the eyes of one's fellows. In a writing contemporary with Blackmore's,[12] by the first great English naturalist, John Ray, it was observed that this too is at once

[11] *An Essay upon False Vertue*, Dublin, 1716: "Of the Desire of Glory that most resembles TRUE VERTUE," p. 22.

[12] In fact, apparently a little earlier, in *Three Physico-Theological Treatises*, 1692; but the quotation following is from the third edition, 1713, p. 429.

a benign and an irrational "passion" providentially bestowed upon man to make up for the deficiency in him of the pure love of virtue.

> I cannot but admire the Wisdom and Goodness of God, in implanting such a Passion in the Nature of Man, as Shame, to no other Use or Purpose, that I can imagine, then to restrain him from vicious and shameful actions. A Passion, I call it, because the Body, as in other Passions, suffers from it, and that in a peculiar manner; it causing a sudden Motion of the Blood to the outward Parts, especially of the Face, which is called Blushing, and a Dejection of the Eyes. If you ask me what Shame is, I answer, it is an ungrateful and afflictive sense of Soul, proceeding from Dishonour. Now Dishonour is nothing else but men's ill opinion of me, or Dislike and condemnation of my Actions, some way declared and manifested to me; which, why I should have such an Abhorrence of, and why it should be so grievous and tormenting to me, there seems to be not a sufficient Ground and Foundation in the Nature of the Thing, supposing such as have this Opinion have neither Power nor Will to hurt my Body, but only in the Ordination of God, who hath so made our Natures, to secure our Innocency and withhold us from the commission of what is disgraceful and ignominious.

Young's *Love of Fame the Universal Passion,* as outlined in the preceding lecture, was primarily a book of satires, devoted to ridiculing and decrying the innumerable manifestations of this human weakness, but it surprisingly concludes with a palinode. The "love of fame" is, after all, Young's readers are now assured, of heavenly origin; it is strongest

in the noblest souls; it is the component of human nature
to which social order and civilization are due, since, but
by virtue of it, the good which the individual most desires
for himself can be attained only through conduct that is
approved by other men. You obviously must not, for
example, if you seek "fame," make jokes at other men's
expense, at least in their presence; for

> The *fame* men give is for the joy they find;
> *Dull* is the jester, when the joke's unkind.[13]

But, unhappily, Young is compelled to admit, this passion
which was meant to be "the flaming minister of virtue" has
sometimes "set up false gods and wrong'd her high descent."
Men have come to take pride in bad qualities as well as
good—presumably, though Young hardly makes this clear,
because the standards which social groups apply in award-
ing praise are often wrong standards, or because the individual may gratify his own vanity by conduct which is *not*
beneficial to society (i.e., in our terminology, self-esteem
and approbativeness may conflict, and the former prevail).
At all events, the solution, he tells us, is not to attempt to
expel this passion from the mind, for that is hopeless, but to
direct it upon good ends by making praise once more con-
ditional upon utility.

> The *true* ambition there alone resides,
> Where justice vindicates, and wisdom guides;
> Where *inward* dignity joins outward state,
> Our *purpose* good, as our achievement great;

---

[13] *Op. cit.*, Sat. II, p. 30.

Where publick *blessings* publick praise attend,
Where glory is our *motive,* not our end.[14]

Young does not tell us how this is to be accomplished; but for some political and social philosophers later in the century, that became precisely the crucial problem.

Christian Wolff, regarded by his contemporaries as the foremost German philosopher in the decades 1720-1750, declared "glory" (which for him meant both the desire for and the attainment of distinction or fame) to be the spur which incites to all notable achievements, apart from any hope of gain.

Nothing pre-eminently great has ever been done in the world which did not flow from glory as its source. . . . This proposition cannot be sufficiently commended; let it be turned over in the mind again and again. Anyone who has ever been able to enjoy glory attributes to it by no means the least part of his happiness. If you use it rightly, that other most delightful emotion which we have called self-satisfaction (*acquiescentia in seipso*) shows itself to be the companion of this one.

Nevertheless Wolff warns against the danger of being led by pride into excessive ambition.[15]

One of the most ardent praisers of the love of praise was Vauvenargues. "If men," he wrote, "had not loved glory, they would not have had enough wit nor enough virtue to merit it." "Glory has filled the world with virtues, and like a kindly sun, it covers the earth with flowers and fruits."

---

[14] *Ibid.,* p. 172.
[15] *Psychologia Empirica* (1732), ed. of 1779, p. 325.

"Ambition, in the great, renders them accessible, hard-working, honest, serviceable, and makes them practise the virtues which they lack by nature—a merit often superior to these virtues themselves, since it is usually proof of *une ame forte*."[16]

In 1742 William Melmoth the younger, in his *Fitzosborne's Letters,* Letter XVIII, confesses that there are some who have represented this passion "as inconsistent with both reason and religion," for example, Wollaston, but to this "sentiment" he cannot subscribe. Even though all that has been said of the irrationality and vanity of the craving for renown may be true, "yet it would not necessarily follow, that true philosophy would banish [this desire] from the human breast." It may be that it is born of an illusion, a "mistake," but to see things as they truly and in themselves are would not always, perhaps, be of advantage to us in the intellectual world, any more than in the natural. And so, after repeating the usual arguments for and illustrations of the social utility of the passion, Melmoth too concludes that it is

a very dangerous attempt, to endeavour to lessen the motives of right conduct, or to raise any suspicion concerning their solidity. While some men are willing to wed virtue for her personal charms, others are engaged to take her for the sake of her expected dowry; and since her followers and admirers have so little hope from her in the present, it were pity, methinks, to reason them out of any imagined advantage in recreation.

[16] *Réflexions et maximes,* Nos. 152, 495, 371.

Pope, a poet who in his way of thinking and poetic style was certainly utterly different from Milton, nevertheless was not less emphatic in asserting that the love of praise—but in his case solely of human praise—was the force which causes men to scorn the pleasures of the senses and pursue nonegoistic ends. Pride and shame were "happy frailties" which by the wisdom of "Heaven" were "to all ranks apply'd" in its purpose to "disappoint th' effect of every vice," for it is these susceptibilities of man that

> Virtue's ends from vanity can raise,
> Which seeks no int'rest, no reward but praise.[17]

But, as Pope seems here to forget, "vanity" was for him one of the "passions," and the passions, he had told us, are "born to fight" and tend to produce "discord" among men. Here, however, was a "passion" which has the contrary tendency. The desire for praise makes for social concord, since it causes individuals to do what others wish them to do and esteem or admire them for doing. In so far as it influences conduct, it by its very nature serves to realize the same ends as "virtue" itself, and in order to do so it does not need to be "mixed" with the other, the intrinsically evil, passions. Pope, then, had two implicitly distinct conceptions of the way in which the disruptive tendency of all the passions (except one) can be overcome: first, by skillfully combining and counterbalancing them so that as the end-result these "jarring passions" will "of *themselves* create

[17] *Essay on Man*, II, 245-6. Note that the word "vanity" here means "the desire for praise."

th' according music of the well-mixed State"; second, by relying upon the one passion which is *not* "jarring" and disruptive, but intrinsically conducive to good conduct and social peace and harmony. The former conception we noted in Lecture II.[18] But Pope himself made no sharp distinction between the two, since both features of man's constitution were devices used by Heaven to accomplish the same desirable end. Both also served to illustrate Pope's general thesis that the passions and not the Reason are the dynamic "elements of life."

No contrast could, at first sight, seem sharper than that between the comparatively mild and edifying reasonings which I have earlier quoted from Abbadie and the violent and cynical paradoxes (as they appeared to many of his readers) of Bernard de Mandeville two decades later (1716). Yet the two writers were dealing with the same problem and propounding the same answer to it; the difference lies mainly in the manner of approach and presentation. For Mandeville was less original than he seems; he too was the continuer and transmitter of a tradition, as Kaye has pointed out in his admirable edition of *The Fable of the Bees.* He was even less unorthodox than he seems; for his most general paradox, in the subtitle of the book—"Private Vices, Public Benefits"—was simply the converse of the doctrine of human depravity. Theological defenders of that doctrine had, as we have seen, sought to show that even objectively beneficial, socially desirable, actions can be

[18] See above, pp. 42 ff. There is yet a third strain in Pope, incongruous with the second, which we shall note later.

traced to subjective "vices,"—i.e., to supposedly evil and irrational motives in the "heart" of the individual. So be it, says Mandeville. Then evil or irrational motives—"private vices"—can and do produce socially desirable actions—"public benefits"; and man being what by hypothesis he is, the benefits cannot be got in any other way. And this for Mandeville is the important point. That he really considered any motive that has desirable social consequences a "vice" is at least doubtful; but at any rate he usually keeps up a lofty pretense of regarding as evil all the traits of human nature which he at the same time represents as the causes that make civilized society possible. It is, on the other hand, not certain that he thought all their consequences socially desirable; for he is often obviously satirizing the society of his time, and this strain in his writing—though this only— was presumably congenial to the temper of the primitivists. He seems, it must be confessed, chiefly bent upon annoying everybody; he was the universal gadfly, ready to sting all classes of his contemporaries upon whom his wide-ranging attention lighted; and his own convictions are therefore difficult to determine. But at all events he surpassed all of his precursors and most of his successors in the ingenuity and detail with which he sought to trace the necessary connection between what had usually been considered "private vices" and what were commonly regarded as "public benefits." The particular "vice" from which nearly all the "benefits" flow is, for him, "pride." And the chief of the "public benefits" resulting from it is nothing less than the existence of human morality itself. By "pride" Mandeville means, for the most part, approbativeness as a minister to self-esteem.

It is this that is the "origin of virtue."[19] This to him, of course, was the most pleasing paradox of all, that "virtue" itself should be the child of what had commonly been called a "vice"—and, according to an age-old tradition, the worst of the vices.

His argument for this thesis takes the form of an account of the genesis of morality, both in the history of mankind and in the development of the individual. In the primitive state of nature men are assumed to have been devoid of moral ideas; it was no Golden Age. Like other "untaught animals" our earliest ancestors were "only solicitous of pleasing themselves, and naturally follow[ed] the bent of their own inclinations, without considering the good or harm that from their being pleased will accrue to others." But, Mandeville by no means denies, men as we now know them do in some measure control their natural impulses and appetites, and they do subordinate private to public interests. How was this strange transformation brought about? Here Mandeville introduces upon the scene, from nowhere in particular, certain "Lawgivers and other wise men," who, recognizing the evils of the purely natural state and "labouring for the establishment of society," set about finding a means of controlling the behavior of the animal man. The Lawgivers' problem was to find a "reward" which would seem to men sufficient to compensate them for the "trouble of self-denial" and the unpleasantness of self-control. And in the constitution of this animal the Lawgivers found a peculiar trait which was singularly to their purpose:

[19] In the "Enquiry into the Origin of Moral Virtue," 1714; *The Fable of the Bees*, Kaye ed., I, pp. 41 ff.

They thoroughly examined all the Strength and Frailties of our Nature, and observing that none were either so savage as not to be charm'd with Praise or so despicable as patiently to bear Contempt, they justly concluded that Flattery must be the most powerful argument that could be used to human Creatures.[20]

All that was necessary, then, was to accustom men to bestow praise upon the kinds of acts and attitudes which the Lawgivers wished to promote, and contempt upon their opposites.

In accomplishing this, the Lawgivers were assisted by a kindred propensity of men, emulation, initially in the form of a susceptibility to pleasure in feeling themselves as a species superior to other animals. This same notion, that self-esteem first manifested itself as a gratifying feeling of the generic superiority of *homo sapiens* to the other creatures, was, it will be remembered, adopted by Rousseau in the *Second Discourse* some forty years later; it is, I think, not unlikely that he borrowed it from Mandeville. But Rousseau makes very little use of it. According to him, the sense of racial superiority simply passed over directly into emulation between individuals, the desire to think of oneself as superior to some or to the generality of other persons. Rousseau was not seeking, in this supposed *premier mouvement d'orgueil,* for the origin of morality; he was, on the contrary, seeking for the initial stage of the progressive immorality of human behavior. Mandeville, however, having precisely the opposite thesis to maintain, gives a subtler turn to the idea. He supposes that his imaginary Lawgivers

[20] Cf. Kaye's notes, *op. cit.,* p. 42.

seized upon this primary sense in primitive men of their racial superiority to convert it into a desire to show themselves superior to other individuals *by virtue of* the exercise of those capacities whereby man as such is distinguished from the animals—i.e., through intelligence and reason.

> They [the Lawgivers] extolled the excellency of our nature above other animals, and setting forth with unbounded praise the wonders of our Sagacity and Understanding bestow'd a thousand Encomiums on the Rationality of our Souls, by the help of which we are capable of performing the most noble achievements.[21]

And so,

> to introduce an Emulation amongst men, they divided the whole Species into two Classes, vastly differing from one another: The one consisted of abject, low-minded People, that, always hunting after immediate Enjoyment, were wholly incapable of Self-denial, and without regard to the good of others, . . . and made no use of their Rational Faculties but to heighten their Sensual Pleasure. Those vile grov'ling Wretches, they said, were the Dross of their Kind, and having only the Shape of Men, differ'd from Brutes in nothing but their outward Shape. But the other Class was made up of lofty, high-spirited Creatures, that, free from sordid Selfishness, esteem'd the improvement of the Mind to be their fairest Possession; and, setting a true value upon themselves, took no Delight but in embellishing that Part in which their Excellency consisted; such as despising whatever they had in common

[21] *Op. cit.*, Kaye ed., I, p. 43.

with irrational Creatures, . . . and, making a continual
war with themselves to promote the Peace of others,
aim'd at no less than the Publick Welfare.

This, then, says Mandeville, "was (or at least might have
been) the manner after which Savage Man was broke."

> It was not any Heathen Religion or other Idolatrous
> Superstition, that first put man upon crossing his Appetites
> and subduing his dearest Inclinations, but the skilful
> management of wary Politicians; and the nearer we
> search into human Nature, the more we shall be con-
> vinced, that the Moral Virtues are the Political Offspring
> which Flattery begot upon Pride.[22]

The jeering and ironic tone in which Mandeville expressed
all this has prevented most of his critics and commentators
from noticing the logical substance of what he was saying
about the genesis and basis of morality. It *could* be expressed in a much more edifying way: namely, that the
supposititious Lawgivers impressed upon the minds of early
men a feeling of "the dignity of human nature" by virtue of
its rationality and taught them not only to conceive of themselves as rational creatures, but to behave, in some degree,
in the manner which such a conception of themselves seemed
to require; but that this would have been impossible if the
susceptibility to a particular kind of pride had not already
been latent in men, that is, the pride which consists in the
pleasure of thinking of oneself as a member of a race of
which rationality is the distinguishing attribute or the unpleasantness of thinking of oneself as "no better than the

[22] *Ibid.*, p. 51.

beasts." It would be misleading to suggest that Mandeville himself was much impressed with the dignity or rationality of man, or that he was seeking to give his readers a high opinion of their kind. Nevertheless, in the *Enquiry into the Origin of Moral Virtue*, he clearly presupposes that man *is* differentiated from the animals by the possession of reason; and he expressly asserts that a desire to act, or to believe that one is acting, rationally is a distinctively human motive, and that in consequence of this men are, more or less, capable both of the control of the other passions and of the subordination of private to public interests.

The device of the primeval sage or lawgiver deliberately contriving ways to "civilize mankind" seems to us, of course, an absurd one, and it was effectively ridiculed by some of Mandeville's contemporary critics. But it had a literary tradition behind it, it made the story more amusing, and it served his satirical bent by making the whole affair appear as a kind of trickery played upon the naive savages by "wary politicians" for purposes of their own. But in fact Mandeville himself, as he elsewhere makes clear, did not take this feature of his account of the genesis of the moral virtues seriously; it was merely a literary artifice. The transformation of the amoral beast that man originally was into a being capable of morality was not accomplished all at once through the conscious contrivance of a few "wise men," but was in reality, Mandeville recognizes, a long and gradual process: "it is the work of Ages to find out the true Use of the Passions."[23]

[23] Cf. Kaye, *op. cit.*, lxiv, lxvi.

It was not, however, necessary, for the justification of Mandeville's thesis of the moralizing of man through "pride," to resort to conjectures about the early history of the species; it is enough, he observes, to look at the way in which children, who at the beginning are not very different from wild animals, are now moralized and made fit for society. What in this process wise parents and tutors chiefly rely on is the child's latent capacity for pride; appeals to this are, Mandeville thought, far more potent than physical rewards and punishments. To prevent the small boy from crying, which to his elders is an unpleasant noise and spectacle, he is told that big boys do not cry when they are hurt, and as the idea of himself as a big boy is fascinating to him, he represses his natural animal outburst. Hourly, and from many sources, praise and blame are applied to him, or *models* of conduct are set before him—actual ones or heroes of fiction—and they are represented as in the highest degree admirable; and so, wishing above all things to look upon himself as admirable, the child begins, in some degree, to emulate the virtues of these models. Mandeville, however, is somewhat confused as to the relative parts played in this civilizing of the child by the motives of self-esteem and approbativeness. His more frequent emphasis is upon the desire to be actually admired and praised by others; and because he regards being admired and praised as an insubstantial, an unreal value, he tends to use his account of the method of moral education as a further means of satirizing his race—of representing man to himself as an irrational, ridiculous, and self-deceiving creature. Nevertheless, Mandeville is insistent upon the immense social utility of this desire, at least as social utility is usually judged, and upon the intensity of the pleasure which the individual may get from its satisfaction, or from his belief that it is being satisfied.

Mandeville's tone and temper being what they were, it is not surprising that most of the bishops and other clergy who wrote replies to *The Fable of the Bees* were unable to penetrate the spiky crust of paradox and satire in which he had enveloped his idea and see what was significant and true in it. William Law, for example, though he was both a saint and an acute mind, when he deals with "Dr. Mandeville's particular account of the *Origin of Moral Virtue,*" seeks to refute it by a *reductio ad absurdum* which is essentially a caricature.

> You are pleased [he is addressing Mandeville] to impute its origin to *Pride* alone. But if *Pride* be the only foundation of Virtue, then the more Vicious anyone *is,* the more humble he ought to be esteemed; and he who is the most humble is at the greatest distance he can be placed from a moral Virtue. And a perfect Humility (which by most Moralists has been reckoned a Virtue) must according to this Account, render anyone incapable of any Virtue; for such a one not only wants that which you make the only Cause of Virtue, but is possessed of the contrary Quality.[24]

Law here simply caught up Mandeville's crucial word without examining its meaning. Mandeville has *not* said or implied that the most vicious man is the most humble, or *vice versa*. By "pride" he plainly meant two things: a *craving*

[24] Law, in 1723; in *Works*, 1762; 1892 reprint, II, pp. 9-10.

to be able to think well of oneself, and a craving to be well thought of, chiefly as an aid to the former. Leave out the "wary politicians," the innuendos, the ironic by-play, and all the accessories which Mandeville introduced to amuse or horrify his readers, and his general thesis, in the essay in question, comes down to this: that approbativeness and the desire for self-esteem and the aversion from their opposites are the initial and the principal subjective sources, the inner and distinctively human appetencies, from which, in fact, the kind of conduct usually recognized as moral arises; that these are the affective components of human nature through which the interests of other men and the moral standards of a society get their hold upon the conduct of the individual. And *this* was no novelty and, so expressed, was hardly a paradox. It had, as we have seen, been said by more than one before Mandeville, not only by so orthodox and respected a theologian as Abbadie: it was, as we have yet to see, to be repeated after him by other eminent writers who probably had not learned it from Mandeville or, if they had, did not acknowledge their debt to a precursor of such notorious ill-repute.

A great contemporary English moralist who, in personal characteristics and temper and in his general ethical doctrine, was certainly extremely unlike Mandeville, must also be set down among those who saw in approbativeness a nonrational and egoistic but beneficent appetite of man, an indispensable source of what Mandeville called "public benefits." Bishop Butler counts the "desire for esteem" in its necessary effect, as distinct from its intent, among "the public affections or passions," because "the end for which it was given us is to regulate our behaviour towards society, in such a manner as will be of service to our fellow creatures. . . . The object and end" of it "is merely esteem. But the latter can no more be gratified, without contributing to the good of society, than [hunger] can be gratified without contributing to the preservation of the individual."[25]

The passions in general, Voltaire observed in 1734, "are the principal cause of the order which we see to-day upon the earth"; but among these,

It is pride above all that has been the principal instrument with which the fair edifice of society has been built. Scarcely had their needs brought a few men to live in a community, when the shrewdest among them perceived that all these men were born with an indomitable pride as well as an invincible desire for well-being. It was not difficult to persuade them that, if they would do something for the common good of the group at some small cost to their own well-being, their pride would gain ample recompense for this loss. Thus men were early distinguished into two classes: the first, that of those godlike men who sacrifice their self-interest to the public good; the second, that of the wretches who care only for themselves. Everybody thereupon desired, and still desires, to be of the former, though everybody at the bottom of his heart is of the latter; and the most cowardly men and those most abandoned to their own desires cried out the loudest that everything must be sacrificed to the public good. The craving to command, one of the branches of pride, which is as evident in a pedant of a college or a village justice

[25] *Sermons* (1724); 5th ed., 1765, p. 11.

of the peace (*bailli*) as in a Pope and an Emperor, still more potently excites human endeavor to bring men to obey other men. . . . God has wisely endowed us with a pride which can never suffer that other men should hate or despise us. To be an object of contempt to those with whom one lives is a thing that none ever has been, or ever will be, able to endure. It is perhaps the greatest check which nature has placed upon men's injustice; it is by this mutual fear that God has thought best to bind men together.[26]

Voltaire was here manifestly appropriating (without acknowledgment) Mandeville's account of the origin of morality—not even omitting the primeval "Wise Men."

Hume's fundamental thesis must have shocked some of his contemporaries more profoundly than any of the satirists' assertions of the irrationality of the dominant motives of man. For while they had declared that the Reason seldom if ever does in fact control the passions, they had still assumed, in accord with the long dominant tradition, that it should do so, that control was the function for which it was intended; without this assumption, there would have been no point to their satires. But Hume challenged the great tradition of moral philosophy, and asserted that it is a psychological impossibility for the Reason to influence volition.

Nothing is more usual in philosophy, and even in common life, than to talk of the combat of passion and reason, and to assert that men are only so far virtuous as they

[26] *Traité de Metaphysique.*

conform themselves to its dictates. On this method of thinking the greater part of moral philosophy seems to be founded.

But, he continues, "in order to show the fallacy of all this philosophy, I shall endeavor to prove, *first*, that reason alone can never be a motive to any action of the will; and *secondly*, that it can never oppose passion in the direction of the will."[27] Hume does not, of course, mean by this to deny that the understanding has an instrumental use in the determination of conduct. Given a desire for some end, a reasoned knowledge of the relations of cause and effect may show us how to satisfy it by adopting the means without which the end cannot be attained. What he is asserting is that "reason," the knowledge of any kind of truth, is *not* a passion or desire, is not the same psychological phenomenon as liking or *wanting* something; and that a thing can become an end only by being desired. The role of reason consists in judging of propositions as true or false, as in "agreement or disagreement" with the matters of fact to which they refer. "Whatever is not susceptible of this agreement or diagreement, is incapable of being true or false, and can never be an object of our reason." But "our passions, volitions and acts" are "original facts and realities, compleat in themselves. . . . 'Tis impossible, therefore, that they can be either true or false, and be either contrary or conformable to reason."[28] And since reason neither is nor can produce a desire, it cannot even tell us what we should desire, it

[27] *Treatise of Human Nature*, I, iii, 3; p. 413.
[28] *Treatise of Human Nature*, Bk. III, Pt. 1, 1.

cannot evaluate desires; or if it professes to do so, it will only the more clearly reveal its irrelevance and impotence. You either have a desire or you do not; unless you have one, you will never act at all; and a desire can be combatted or overcome, not by reason, but only by another desire.

It is unnecesary to enter into Hume's complicated and over-elaborate analysis of the passions. It is enough for my present purpose to ask whether he attaches any unique importance to those "springs of action" which I have named approbativeness, self-esteem, and emulativeness. Sometimes he is content to suggest that the desire for the approval of others is merely a derivative of self-esteem, as a means of corroborating or correcting our good opinions of our own favorable judgments of ourselves, or our qualities, or behavior; self-admiration is, here, apparently the more fundamental passion, which is common to us and some of the higher animals (dogs and even peacocks, for example). He writes in the *Enquiry Concerning the Principles of Morals*:

> [a] spring of our constitution, that brings a great addition of force to moral sentiments, is the *love of fame; which rules, with such uncontrolled authority, in all generous minds, and is often the grand object of all their designs and undertakings.* By our continual and earnest pursuit of a character, a name, a reputation in the world, we bring our own deportment and conduct frequently in review, and consider how they appear in the eyes of those who approach and regard us. This constant habit of surveying ourselves, as it were, in reflection, keeps alive all the sentiments of right and wrong, and begets, in noble natures, a certain reverence for themselves as well as

others, which is the surest guardian of every virtue. . . .
Our moral sentiment is itself a feeling chiefly of that
nature, and our regard to a character with others seems
to arise only from a care of preserving a character with
ourselves; and in order to attain this end, we find it necessary to prop our tottering judgement on the correspon-
dent approbation of mankind.

Hume, it must be parenthetically observed, falls into some
inconsistencies. If a desire occurring at a certain time in
my consciousness is what Hume says it is, "complete in itself," it requires, for me, no corroboration, and no other
person can be qualified to corroborate the existence in me
of that desire; only a proposition can be corroborated or
refuted, and a desire is, according to Hume, not a proposition. Similar inconsistencies may be seen in his use of the
term "moral sentiments." Is a sentiment a judgment, which
can be true or false, or a desire, which can be neither true
nor false? When he is writing as an earnest moral philoso-
pher-sage to improve the motives and behavior of his readers, he prefixes the adjective "moral" to the noun, and the
term then designates a judgment of values, or what is truly
good or bad, or right or wrong. But when he is writing as
an acute analytical psychologist—which he also was—he
must, in consistency, consider "moral sentiments" simply
as one class of desires, to which the concept of truth or
falsity is inapplicable. But Hume was far from admitting
that we desire the approbation of others *merely* as a means
of "checking" on the correctness of our own "moral sentiments," other men's "sentiments" maybe, though Hume does
not, as some of his contemporaries did, point out that the

"sentiments" of others may be as erroneous as ours. His ethical doctrine (of which I shall treat more fully in Lecture VIII) did not permit him to assert that approbativeness is itself a "virtue," or even a substitute for virtue, i.e., for completely disinterested actions or intentions of action. It is, obviously and undeniably, a self-regarding passion; we desire its gratification because it—or the belief that it is gratified—gives us pleasure, not because it gives pleasure to others; and the same is obviously true of emulativeness. Yet no man ever wrote more copiously and zealously in praise of this passion. If it is not virtue, it is the next thing to it, is difficult to distinguish from it, and always accompanies it. So in one of his essays:

It has always been found, that the virtuous are far from being indifferent to praise; and therefore they have been represented as a set of vain-glorious men, who had nothing in view but the applauses of others. But this . . . is a fallacy. It is very unjust in the world, when they find any tincture of vanity in a laudable action, to depreciate it upon this account, or ascribe it entirely to that motive. The case is not the same with vanity, as with other passions. Where avarice or revenge enters into any seemingly virtuous action, it is difficult for us to determine how far it enters, and it is natural to suppose it the sole actuating principle. But vanity is so closely allied to virtue, and to love the fame of laudable actions approaches so near the love of laudable actions for their own sake, that these passions are more capable of mixture, than any other kinds of affection; and it is almost impossible to have the latter without some degree of the former. Accordingly, we find, that this passion for glory is always warped and varied according to the particular taste or disposition of the mind on which it falls. . . . *To love the glory of virtuous deeds is a sure proof of the love of virtue.*[29]

Though Hume liked to dilate in this edifying manner on the close kinship of approbativeness and virtue, he could also view mankind more realistically; he was well aware that that passion does not manifest itself solely in a quest of "the glory of virtuous deeds," but also in almost countless other ways—that, in fact, all of us find pleasure in thinking that others esteem or admire and applaud us for the possession of any kind of objects or attributes which we take pride in calling "ours." In the *Treatise* he writes:

There are few persons, that are satisfied with their own character, or genius, or fortune, who are not desirous of shewing themselves to the world, and of acquiring the love and approbation of mankind. Now 'tis evident, that the very same qualities and circumstances, which are the causes of pride or self-esteem, are also the causes of vanity or the desire of reputation; and that we always put to view those particulars with which in ourselves we are best satisfied.[30]

In fact, Hume elsewhere implies, there is nothing to which the possessive pronoun "my" can be attached to which this desire for the admiration and applause of others does not

[29] *Philosophical Essays on Morals, Literature, and Politics* (1st Amer. ed., 1817), Vol. I, Essay XI, "Of the Dignity or Meanness of Human Nature," pp. 108-109. Italics mine.

[30] *Treatise of Human Nature*, Book II, Part II, Section 1, pp. 331-332.

extend; it is not merely approval of our moral characters
or behavior that we crave. The

> most obvious and remarkable property [of pride and
> humility] is the vast variety of *subjects*, on which they
> may be plac'd. Every valuable quality of the mind,
> whether of the imagination, judgment, memory or disposi-
> tion; wit, good-sense, learning, courage, justice, integrity;
> all these are the causes of pride; and their opposites of
> humility. Nor are these passions confin'd to the mind,
> but extend their view to the body likewise. A man may be
> proud of his beauty, strength, agility, good mein [*sic*],
> address in dancing, riding, fencing, and of his dexterity in
> any manual business or manufacture. But this is not all.
> The passion looking farther comprehends whatever ob-
> jects are in the least ally'd or related to us. Our country,
> family, children, relations, riches, houses, gardens, horses,
> dogs, cloaths; any of these may become a cause either
> of pride or humility.[31]

Though Hume's reference here is to pride and humility, it
must be remembered that he has elsewhere emphasizd that
self-esteem is always accompanied by approbativeness. "Our
reputation, our character, our name are considerations of
vast weight and importance; and even the other causes of
pride; virtue, beauty and riches; have little influence, when
not seconded by the opinions and sentiments of others."[32]
Nor does Hume neglect the potency of the passion of emulativeness, which is of course a form of the desire for self-
esteem.

[31] *Ibid.*, Book II, Part I, Section II, p. 279.
[32] *Ibid.*, Book II, Part I, Section XI, p. 316.

[There are two principles which] are very conspicuous in human nature. . . . The second principle I shall take notice of is that of *comparison,* or the variation of our judgments concerning objects, according to the proportion they bear to those with which we compare them. We judge more of objects by comparison, than by their intrinsic worth and value; and regard every thing as mean, when set in opposition to what is superior of the same kind. But no comparison is more obvious than that with ourselves; and hence it is that on all occasions it takes place, and mixes with most of our passions.[33]

Hume, like others of the period, obviously had derived some of his ideas concerning the principal motivations of human behavior from Mandeville, though he keeps up a certain air of disapproval even while borrowing from that disreputable author, to whom he clearly refers in the following passage without mentioning his name:

Tho' this progress of the sentiments be *natural,* and even necessary, 'tis certain that it is here forwarded by the artifice of politicians, who, in order to govern men more easily, and preserve peace in human society, have endeavour'd to produce an esteem for justice, and an abhorrence of injustice. This, no doubt, must have its effect; but nothing can be more evident, than that the matter has been carry'd too far by certain writers on morals, who seem to have employ'd their utmost efforts to extirpate all sense of virtue from among mankind. Any artifice of politicians may assist nature in the producing of those sentiments, which she suggests to us, and may even on

[33] *Ibid.,* Book III, Part III, Section II, pp. 592-593.

some occasions, produce alone an approbation or esteem for any particular action; but 'tis impossible it should be the sole cause of the distinction we make betwixt vice and virtue. For if nature did not aid us in this particular, 'twould be in vain for politicians to talk of *honourable* or *dishonourable, praiseworthy* or *blameable.* These words wou'd be perfectly unintelligible, and wou'd no more have any idea annex'd to them, than if they were of a tongue perfectly unknown to us. The utmost politicians can perform is, to extend the natural sentiments beyond their original bounds; but still nature must furnish the materials, and give us some notion of moral distinctions. . . . As publick praise and blame increase our esteem for justice; so private education and instruction contribute to the same effect. For as parents easily observe, that a man is the more useful, both to himself and others, the greater degree of probity and honour he is endow'd with; and that those principles have greater force, when custom and education assist interest and reflexion: For these reasons they are induc'd to inculcate on their children, from their earliest infancy, the principles of probity, and teach them to regard the observance of those rules, by which society is maintain'd, as worthy and honourable, and their violation as base and infamous. By this means the sentiments of honour may take root in their tender minds, and acquire such firmness and solidity, that they may fall little short of those principles, which are the most essential to our natures, and the most deeply radicated in our internal constitution. . . . What farther contributes to encrease their solidity, is the interest of our reputation, after the opinion, *that a merit or demerit attends justice or injustice,* is once firmly establish'd

among mankind. There is nothing, which touches us more
nearly than our reputation, and nothing on which our
reputation more depends than our conduct, with relation
to the property of others. For this reason, every one, who
has any regard to his character, or who intends to live on
good terms with mankind, must fix an inviolable law to
himself, never, by any temptation, to be induc'd to violate
those principles, which are essential to a man of probity
and honour.[34]

The reader will observe that these objections, apparently
to Mandeville, had been in fact expressed by that writer
himself.

Adam Smith in his *Theory of Moral Sentiments*, 1759, the
most original and systematic eighteenth-century inquiry
concerning the motivations of human behavior, expressed
the same opinion as most of his contemporaries about the
supreme potency of approbativeness, and unlike some of
them, he saw both sides of the picture—the negative side,
the fear of disapprobation and contempt, and the positive
side, the craving for the esteem of others.

[The] love of virtue [is] the noblest and best passion of
human nature. The love of true glory [is] a passion
inferior, no doubt, to the former, but which in dignity
appears to come immediately after it.[35]

And again:

Nature, when she formed man for society, endowed him

[34] *Ibid.*, Book II, Part II, Section III, pp. 500-501.
[35] *Theory of Moral Sentiments*, p. 44.

with an original desire to please, and an original aversion to offend his brethren. She taught him to feel pleasure in their favourable, and pain in their unfavourable, regard. She rendered their approbation most flattering and most agreeable to him for its own sake, and their disapprobation most motifying and most offensive. . . .[36]

"Compared with the contempt of mankind, all other evils are easily supported;" but also, "what of all things [every individual] has the greatest desire to do" is "to act so as that the impartial spectator may enter into the principles of his conduct"—that is to say, may approve of the motives prompting it; to this end he "must humble the arrogance of his self-love, and bring it down to something other men can go along with."[37] To "enter into" or "go along with" the judgments of others means, in Smith's terminology, to approve what they approve and to disapprove what they disapprove.

The desire for the esteem and admiration of other people, when for qualities and talents which are the natural and proper objects of esteem and admiration, is the real love of true glory—a passion which, if not the very best passion of human nature, is certainly one of the best. . . . *The great secret of education is to direct vanity to proper objects.* Never suffer him [one's son] to value himself upon trivial accomplishments. But do not always discourage his pretensions to those that are of real importance.

Thus Smith also, near the end of the century, found ap-

[36] *Ibid.*, pp. 144-5.
[37] *Op. cit.*, 1st edition, pp. 146 and 182.

probativeness one of the best passions of men and indispensable in the proper education of the young.

Towards the end of the century Immanuel Kant, in his *Conjectures concerning the Beginning of Human History* (*Muthmasslicher Anfang der Menschengeschichte*), 1786, took up the problem which had long before been broached by Mandeville. It seems evident that it was suggested to him by a reading of *The Fable of the Bees*,[38] though Kant must have been repelled by its satirical tone and by its failure to offer any historical evidence on what was essentially a question of historical fact. Nevertheless, Kant's own formulation of the problem was based upon the same initial assumption, and his own proposed solution of it was based upon the same antecedent assumption—namely, that in the first phase of the history of our species, man was simply an unsocial and unintelligent animal destitute of any ideas of moral distinctions and of any sense of moral obligation, a creature "human" only in a biological sense. The problem therefore was: how, through the supervention or evocation of what originally latent and undeveloped intellectual powers and affective propensities was this amoral animal transformed into man as we now know him, "as a moral creature," *ein sittliches Geschöpf*, able and (more or less) inclined to subordinate his inherited animal cravings to the requirements of membership in a genuine society? This,

[38] For evidence of Kant's acquaintance with Mandeville's writings and also an interesting account of the influence of Mandeville in Germany in the eighteenth century, cf. the appendix "References to Mandeville's Work" in F. B. Kaye's edition of *The Fable of the Bees*, Vol. II, pp. 418 ff.

then—which, it will be remembered, was the problem in practical psychology which Mandeville's primeval "Wise Men" were supposed to have solved—was Kant's problem. And his solution of it was almost, if not quite, the same as theirs.

> A craving to inspire in others esteem (*Achtung*) for ourselves, through good behavior (repression of that which could arouse in them a poor opinion [*Geringschätzung*] of us), is the real basis of all true sociality (*Geselligkeit*), and, moreover, it gave the first hint (*Wink*) of the development of man as a moral creature—a small beginning, but an epoch-making one, since it gives man's way of thinking a wholly new direction, and is therefore more important than the whole series (of which we cannot foresee the end) of extensions of civilization (*Cultur*) which followed from it.[39]

None of Kant's predecessors had voiced the praise of approbativeness in quite such high terms, and he was one of the few philosophers of his period who—though he did not accept the biological theory of the tranformation of species —did declare that, once created, the human species had passed through a long process of moral evolution.[40]

[39] *Kant's Werke*, Prussian Academy edition, VIII, p. 113.
[40] See the writer's article on Kant in the volume entitled *Forerunners of Darwin*, 1959, p. 190 f.

Lecture VI ❦ ❦ ❦

APPROBATIVENESS AND "PRIDE" IN
POLITICAL AND ECONOMIC THOUGHT

What the last lecture showed was that in most of the observations on the dominant motives of man which were there cited, these seventeenth- and eighteenth-century writers were seeking, and believed they had found, effective substitutes for "reason" and "virtue" in the control of human behavior—substitutes it seemed imperatively necessary to find because "reason" and "virtue", though they doubtless should, seldom if ever do, direct men's conduct. But the substitutes—approbativeness or self-esteem or emulation or all three together—are, by the beneficent dispensation of Providence, capable of producing the same effects in outward conduct as reason and virtue themselves.

1. Manifestly, from these premises the political philosopher should be able to deduce important practical conclusions. But just what conclusions? One answer was given by Montesquieu. He observed that the great advantage of monarchical governments, with a hierarchy of ranks and orders, is that in them "politics can achieve great things with as little virtue as possible." For the "spring of action" in monarchies is "honor," the desire for "preferences and distinctions"; and this provides an adequate substitute for "political virtue. It can inspire the finest actions; it can, combined with the force of law, lead to the end of government as well as virtue itself."

[Doubtless,] philosophically speaking, it is a false honor which moves all parts of the State; but this false honor is as useful to the public as the true would be to whatever individuals might possess it. And is it not a great thing to oblige men to perform all the actions that are difficult and demand energy, without any recompense except the fame (*bruit*) attaching to such actions?[1]

In democracies, on the other hand, according to Montesquieu, though this spring of action need not be wholly absent, another and very different motivation is absolutely essential: it is "political virtue," that is, "a constant preference of the public interest to one's own." There must be no rivalry among citizens for personal advantages; *l'amour de la démocratie est celui de l'égalité;* individual "ambition is limited to the sole desire, the sole happiness, of rendering to one's country greater services than other citizens."[2] This contrast between the motives upon which the two systems must respectively depend for their success and permanence, I think, did not imply for most eighteenth-century readers, the superiority of equalitarian democracy. If you could depend upon civic virtue to make a political system work satisfactorily, that would doubtless be the ideal form of government; but since it was commonly assumed that you can't, it followed that you will do better to rely upon a less exalted but far more potent and less rare spring of action in men, the desire for honors, distinctions, recognized superiority, which, properly utilized, can bring about the same desirable results.

[1] *De l'esprit des lois*, Bk. III. ch. 6-7.
[2] *Ibid.*, Bk. V, ch. 3.

Even Rousseau, though he of course belongs mainly among the decriers of "pride," insists, in the wisest, though unhappily not the most influential, of his political writings, the *Considerations on the Government of Poland,* that approbativeness is the motive upon which the statesman must chiefly rely for the good regulation of society and points out the futility of legislation which seeks to prevent acts which are not in fact generally disapproved. One could wish that our own statesmen had pondered the following passage of Rousseau before launching on a certain "noble" but short-lived experiment:

Prohibition of the things that ought not to be done is an inept and vain expedient, unless you begin by making them hated and despised; and the reprobation of the law is always ineffectual except when it comes to the support of the [prevailing] judgment. Anyone who endeavors to *instituer un peuple* should know how to *dominer les opinions,* [i.e., approbations and disapprobations] and through them to govern the passions of men.

Of all political figures of the eighteenth century, the one upon whom this complex of ideas seems to have made the deepest impression, and by whom it was most earnestly applied to the practical problems of his time, was the first Vice President of the United States. In 1790, John Adams published, at first anonymously, in the *Gazette of the United States* at Philadelphia, a series of papers entitled *Discourses on Davila.* It was, if I may put it so, a very Adamsy performance; for though apparently designed to influence American opinion on the political issues of the moment, it consisted mainly of thirty-two long chapters of quotations or summaries of a *History of the Civil Wars in France* (i. e., the wars of the sixteenth century) by an Italian, Henrico Caterino Davila, with occasional interspersed comments by Adams himself. But in the midst of this historical matter he interpolated twelve chapters[3] of thoughts on "the constitution of the human mind," which are simply a disquisition on the all-importance in human life of emulative approbativeness—variously called by him "the passion for distinction," the individual's "desire to be seen, heard, talked of, approved and respected by the people about him and within his knowledge," "emulation," "the love of praise," the "desire of the attention, consideration, and congratulations of others." Adams had read Young's *Love of Fame,* Pope, Voltaire, Rousseau, Dr. Johnson, Adam Smith's *Theory of the Moral Sentiments,* and quotes from them all; he had probably read Mandeville and Hobbes, though he does not quote these less respectable authors. His treatise on human nature is thus a recapitulation and elaboration of nearly all the themes of which examples have already been cited from his predecessors, but with inferences from them pertinent to the problems of the infant Republic of the West. A summary of his argument must therefore be largely a repetition of ideas already expounded and illustrated. But they were here brought together in a more complete and connected pattern, and Adam's expression of them has a historical interest of its own and must not be omitted from this history.

[3] *The Life and Works of John Adams,* 1851, (VI), pp. 232 ff.

Adams equals any of his precursors, and outdoes some of them, in insisting upon the universality and supreme potency of "the passion for distinction" in man.

This propensity, in all its branches, is a principal source of the virtues and vices, the happiness and misery of human life; and . . . the history of mankind is little more than a simple narration of its operation and effects. . . . The desire of esteem is as real a want of nature as hunger; and the neglect and contempt of the world as severe a pain as gout and stone. It sooner and oftener produces despair and a detestation of existence . . . Every personal quality, every blessing of fortune, is cherished in proportion to its capacity of gratifying this universal affection for the esteem, the sympathy, admiration and congratulations of the public.[4]

It is, in short, "the great leading passion of the soul,"[5] and "the theory of education and the science of government may be all reduced to the same simple principle, and be all comprehended in the knowledge of the means of actively conducting, controlling, and regulating the emulation and ambition of its citizens."[6]

Yet it is, Adams admits, a strange and irrational component of human nature: "What a folly is it!" he exclaims (quoting Pope). "On a selfish system, what are the thoughts, passions, sentiments of mankind to us?" Through this desire, "men of all sorts . . . are chained down to an incessant servitude to their fellow-creatures; . . . they are really con-

[4] *Ibid.*, p. 234.
[5] *Ibid.*, p. 246.
[6] *Ibid.*, p. 247.

stituted, by their own vanity, slaves to mankind."[7] But
though it is thus a kind of trick played by "Nature" upon
man's egotism, it is a beneficent trick. For, "as Nature intended men for society, she has endowed them with passions,
appetites and propensities calculated . . . to render them
useful to each other in their social connections. There is
none more essential and remarkable" than this desire of
every man "to be observed, considered, esteemed, praised,
beloved, and admired by his fellows."[8]

The six terms in the clause last quoted are obviously not
synonyms and were not used as such by Adams; they designated for him several species of a common genus, which in
one passage he takes pains to discriminate. He was a more
careful and acute analytical psychologist than any of those
who had previously written on the same theme. While the
generic desire underlying all these motivations is "the passion for distinction," it has three varieties or grades. In
some men it takes the form merely of a desire for "attention," i. e., notoriety or celebrity, regardless of the means
by which it may be attained, and may manifest itself in
conspicuous crimes or extravagant vices—the vanity of the
criminal "big-shot," as our current slang might say.

> The greater number, however, search for distinction,
> neither by vices nor by virtues; but by the means which
> common sense and every day's experience show, are most
> likely to obtain it; by riches, by family records, by play,
> and other frivolous personal accomplishments. But there
> are a few, and God knows, but a few, who aim at some-

[7] *Ibid.*, p. 245.
[8] *Ibid.*, p. 232.

thing more. They aim at approbation as well as attention; at esteem as well as consideration; and at admiration and gratitude, as well as congratulation. Admiration is, indeed, the complete idea of approbation, congratulation, and wonder, united.[9]

It is, I think, uncommonly interesting to picture a busy and influential political figure, in a difficult and highly controversial period of our history, thus sitting down to do a little psychologizing for himself, and to give precise meanings to the terms which he uses. Nor does Adams stop with drawing these distinctions; he goes on—being an Adams—to note the dangers attendant upon even the third form of the passion. It is in those persons who are inspired by it that "most of the great benefactors of mankind" are found. "But for our humiliation we must still remember that in these esteemed, beloved and adored characters, the passion . . . is a passion still; and therefore, like all other human desires, unlimited and insatiable. No man was ever contented with any given share of this human adoration. . . . Man constantly craves for more, even when he has no rival."[10] But when he sees a rival gaining more than himself of this popular acclaim, he feels "a mortification . . . and a resentment of an injustice, as he thinks it. These feelings are other names for jealously and envy; and altogether, they produce some of the keenest and most tormenting of all sentiments."[11] It would be unjust to suppose that in all of these observations Adams was drawing a portrait of himself; but in the final

[9] *Ibid.*, p. 248.
[10] *Ibid.*, pp. 248-249.
[11] *Ibid.*, p. 249.

clause he was, there is reason to think, not unmindful of an emotional experience of his own.[12] It must be added that, though Adams here discriminated these varieties of the "passion for distinction" and their respective consequences, he in many other passages spoke of all of them as normally concomitant in the same persons and conceived of the great majority of mankind—not merely "a few"—as habitually actuated by the desire "to be observed, considered, esteemed, praised, beloved, and admired by their fellows." "It is the only adequate instrument of order and subordination in society, and alone commands effectual obedience to laws, since without it neither human reason, nor standing armies, would ever produce great effect."[13]

It follows that this strongest of human cravings must be the chief object of the attention of the political philosopher and the statesman; "it is the principal end of government to regulate this passion, which in its turn becomes a principal means of government."[14] Adams too, it will be seen, does not think that you can depend upon reason or upon civic virtue as the operating forces of a political society. True, "there is in human nature," he grants, such a thing as "simple Benevolence, or an affection for the good of others; but alone it is not a balance for the selfish affections. Nature, then, has kindly added to Benevolence, the desire for reputation, in order to make us good members of society."[15] True, also, that "Nature has enjoined" upon the individual

[12] See note 18, below.
[13] *Ibid.*, p. 234.
[14] *Ibid.*, p. 234.
[15] *Ibid.*, p. 234.

the duty of respecting "the rights of others as much as his own. But reasoning as abstruse as this . . . would not occur to all men." This injunction of the moral law of nature has therefore had inseparably attached to its observance or disregard the most effective of all rewards and punishments, "the esteem and admiration" or "the neglect and contempt of others."[16]

The political superiority of the Romans, among the peoples of antiquity, was, in Adams's opinion, due to their grasp of the importance of emulation:

Has there [he asks] ever been a nation who understood the human heart better than the Romans, or made a better use of the passion for consideration, congratulation and distinction? . . . *Distinctions of conditions,* as well as of ages, were made by difference of clothing. . . . The chairs of ivory; the lictors; . . . the crowns of gold, of ivory, of flowers; . . . their orations; and their triumphs; everything in religion, government and common life, was parade, representation and ceremony. Everything was addressed to the emulation of the citizens, and everything was calculated to attract the attention, to allure the consideration, and excite the congratulations of the people; to attach their hearts to individual citizens according to their merit; and to their lawgivers, magistrates, and judges, according to their rank, station and importance to the state. And this was in the true spirit of republics, in which form of government there is no other consistent method of preserving order or procuring submission to the laws.[17]

[16] *Ibid.,* p. 234.
[17] *Ibid.,* p. 243. Here, it will be observed, Adams reverses the

When Adams turns to the bearing of his political psychology upon the new Constitution which he is (mainly) defending, he finds it lacking in this respect, in comparison with the Roman. The Constitution did *not* make much provision for attaching outward marks of distinction to "merit" or public service. Presidents and Senators do not wear different garments from the rest of us, or attach medals or similar emblems to their persons (though military officers do). The Constitution did however—and this to him was the best thing about it—utilize emulation to restrain the evils arising *from* emulation and from other passions; in short, it set up a system of checks and balances, first of all by establishing a bicameral Congress, so that each house would be prompted by emulation to resist the encroachments of the other: "a legislature, in one assembly, can have no other termination than in civil dissension, feudal anarchy, or simple monarchy." The Declaration of Rights adopted by the Continental Congress on October 14, 1774, of which Adams—himself not innocent of emulation as against Jefferson—claimed the authorship, and which he regarded as more important than the Declaration of Independence, had declared "it indispensably necessary that the constituent branches of the legislature should be independent of one another."[18] But this was not enough; there must be "an inde-

---

thesis of Montesquieu concerning the "principles" of democracy and monarchy, respectively.

[18] *Ibid.*, pp. 277-8. Adams intensely resented the transfer to Jefferson of the "glory" which he thought due to himself. In 1813 he was still complaining about it: "Such are the caprices of fortune. This declaration of rights was drawn up by the little John

pendent executive authority, such as that in our government, to be a third branch as a mediator or arbitrator between them," and an independent judiciary. "The essence of free government consists in an effectual control of rivalries"—or, at he might better have concluded from his premises, of rivalries *by* rivalries. Here, of course, he is explicitly recognizing the fact, pointed out in Lecture II, that the Constitution was simply an application of the method of counterpoise to the problem of government. But for him the principal motive upon which the effectiveness of the counterpoise depended was not the self-interest of economic groups or any of the other springs of action mentioned by Madison, but the competitive passion for individual distinction. For this negative utilization of that passion Adams thought that the Constitution had pretty well provided.

He did not, however, regard the Constitution as perfect; but his further political deductions from the general premise of the all-importance of "emulation" are confused and obscure, because different considerations about it are manifestly playing upon his mind. Obviously, one cannot make use of this passion without publicly recognizing inequalities among men; and Adams clearly felt the American system to be defective because it had in it too much of the French

Adams. The mighty Jefferson, by the Declaration of Independence, carried away the glory of the great and the little" (*ibid.*, footnote). Though Adams apparently did not attribute this to any deliberate filching of his own fame by Jefferson, his almost obsessing feeling of a rivalry for "glory" between himself and the Virginian was perhaps not unrelated to his death-bed exclamation: "Thomas Jefferson still lives."

equalitarianism. In some passages, therefore, he appears to argue for a hereditary aristocracy of "families distinguished by property, honors, and privileges."[19] To raise himself and his posterity to noble rank will be a potent incentive to the gifted and ambitious man;[20] and the existence of such a class, in any case, provides an additional check against despotism or usurpation on the part of the head of the state. Adams, in this mood, devotes a whole chapter to quotations from that "great teacher of morality and politics," Shakespeare, in *Troilus and Cressida,* depicting the moral and social "chaos" which would result if "Degree," that is, hierarchical order, were abolished. But he then bethinks himself of another side to the question; *hereditary* aristocracies in practice usually become idle and frivolous and, if possessed of political power, oppress "the people." A check against this in turn must be embodied in the political system; in our Constitution Adams thought it was provided for through a lower house of Congress, elected by popular vote. But then—turning back again to the first side of the puzzle— Adams is sure that the people are not the proper fountains of honor. For the problem of good government is to make emulation useful by attaching distinction, and therefore rank or public office, to *real* merit; and of this the multitude can never be a competent judge.

> All civilized free nations have found, by experience, the necessity of separating from the body of the people, and even from the legislature, the distribution of honors, and

[19] *Ibid.,* pp. 250-251.
[20] *Ibid.,* p. 271.

conferring it on the executive authority of government. When the emulation of citizens looks up to one point, . . . you may hope for uniformity, consistency and subordination; but when they look up to different individuals, or assemblies, or councils, you may expect all the deformities, eccentricities, and confusion, of the Polemic system.[21]

It was this passage that, not unintelligibly, gave rise to the charge that Adams in the *Discourses* was an "advocate for monarchy"—a charge which, as he wrote some twenty years later, "powerfully operated to destroy [his] popularity." But, in fact, he was wavering between different conclusions, all suggested to him by a common premise. He was not quite able to make up his mind as to precisely what *would* be an ideal system relying for order and efficiency upon the workings of "emulation." However, the general thesis which he was certain about and was seeking to establish is summed up in these words:

Emulation, next to self-preservation, will ever be the great spring of human actions, and the *balance* of a well-ordered government will alone be able to prevent that emulation from degenerating into dangerous ambition, irregular rivalries, destructive factions, wasting seditions, and bloody civil wars.[22]

2. Thus there was a very large and respectable body of opinion holding that "pride," usually in the sense of approbativeness, is the necessary substitute for "virtue" and the

[21] *Ibid.*, p. 256.
[22] *Ibid.*, p. 279.

motive upon which the good behavior of men depends, and must depend. But it was also evident that a motive so potent and so ubiquitous must manifest itself in the economic order. When its economic aspects were discussed, however, attention shifted from simple approbativeness to a special form of emulation—the craving for distinction based upon the possession of economic goods. Upon the economic effects of "pride" in this general sense numerous writers in our period had a good deal to say. And on this matter also, some of them anticipated a thesis which, if I am not mistaken, has often been supposed to be a novelty of the twentieth century.

At the turn of the century Thorstein Veblen published a work that was destined to celebrity and that constituted, as many of its critics remarked, one of the most subtle and original of American contributions to economic theory— *The Theory of the Leisure Class.* It was primarily a psychological inquiry into the principal motives of the acquisition and expenditure of wealth. The classical economics, Veblen pointed out, usually had described the end of acquisition and accumulation as the "consumption" of the goods acquired—including, of course, under consumption, the satisfaction not only of the consumer's physical wants but also of "his so-called higher wants—spiritual, intellectual, aesthetic, or what not, the latter class of wants being served indirectly by an expenditure of goods, after the fashion familiar to all economic readers." But, observed Veblen,

It is only when taken in a sense far removed from its naive meaning that consumption of goods can be said to afford the incentive from which accumulation invariably proceeds. The motive that lies at the root of ownership is emulation; and the same motive of emulation continues active in the further development of the institution to which it has given rise. . . . The possession of wealth confers honour; it is an invidious distinction. Nothing equally cogent can be said for the consumption of goods, nor for any other conceivable motive of acquisition, and especially not for any incentive to the accumulation of wealth.[23]

Thus economic values are, for the most part, prestige values; once beyond the level of subsistence and physical comfort, economic goods are considered "goods" because their possession and conspicuous expenditure—or conspicuous waste —gratify the desire for distinction, honor, deference, or one or another form of the craving for recognized superiority. It is in the light of this fundamental psychological fact, Veblen maintained, that most of the phenomena of the economic life of a modern industrial society are to be understood; and from the same theorem he drew a number of striking corollaries—among them, that this human craving can never be satisfied in any regime of economic equality, and, in fact, can never be satisfied at all; since the desire is not for any particular sum of possessions, but always for *more* possessions than others have, it can never reach a final limit.

However widely, or equally, or "fairly," it may be distributed, no general increase of the community's wealth

[23] *Theory of the Leisure Class*, 1905, pp. 25 f.

can make any approach to satiating this need, the ground of which is the desire of every one to excel everyone else in the accumulation of goods. If . . . the incentive to accumulation were the want of subsistence or physical comfort, then the aggregate economic wants of a community might conceivably be satisfied at some point in the advance of industrial efficiency; but since the struggle is substantially a race for reputability on the basis of an invidious comparison, no approach to a definitive attainment is possible.[24]

But in all this Veblen was merely repeating and elaborating propositions which may be described as commonplaces of the late seventeenth and the eighteenth centuries—though there is, so far as I know, no reason to suppose that he was aware of this fact. Writers of that period—whether theologians, satirists or philosophers—who were preoccupied with the analysis of "pride" and of its social effects frequently pointed out that that passion, construed either as emulative self-esteem or, more often, as emulative approbativeness, engenders desires for economic goods which have subjective value only as means of distinction—because some or most other people do not have them, or because other people admire or look up to or envy those who do have them. They pointed out that these desires are essentially limitless, and that they are obviously inconsistent with equality.

Thus La Placette wrote in his *Traité de l'orgueil* (1693) :

It is certain that the cause of our love for all these things

[24] *Ibid.*, p. 32.

[possessions, fine clothes, handsome furniture, etc.] is
not so much the utility or pleasure which we find in
them, as the glory which comes from them. There are
very few of them which do not have inconveniences connected with them, of which one would rid oneself if it
were not for this consideration. . . . Without it would
anyone go to so much trouble as we do for cleanliness
and fine clothing? Should we dress as we do if we sought
only comfort and protection against cold or heat?[25]

Mandeville's *Fable of the Bees,* insofar as it is concerned
with economic matters, has for its main theme the dependence of wealth upon "pride." A "hive" in which that motive
was lacking might subsist in modest comfort, everyone being
content with little, but it could never grow rich and powerful. For increase of wealth presupposes increase of desires
for economic goods, and it is from pride that such desires
mainly spring. The "haughty Moralists," says Mandeville,
"conclude that without Pride and Luxury, the same things
might be eat, wore, and consum'd; the same Number of
Handicrafts and Artificers employ'd, and a Nation be every
way as flourishing as where those Vices are the most pre-
dominant." The falsity of this conclusion Mandeville undertakes to prove at length. The truth is that "for the Support
of Trade there can be nothing equivalent to Pride."[26]

Young, in one of his Satires, in a more moralizing tone,
set forth the ecomonic effects of pride as follows:

Nature is frugal, and her wants are few;

[25] *Tr. de l'orgueil,* p. 41.
[26] *Op. cit.,* ed. Kaye, Remark M, pp. 25-26.

> Those few wants answer'd, bring sincere delights;
> But fools create themselves new appetites:
> Fancy and pride, seek things at vast expence,
> Which relish not to *reason,* nor to *sense.*

Expensive things, Young notes, are valued just because they *are* expensive; the ability to pay for them is a social distinction:

> Italian music's sweet, because 'tis dear;
> Their *vanity* is tickled, not their ear;
> Their tastes would lessen, if the prices fell.[27]

But was this tendency of pride to increase *ad indefinitum* the desire for possessions to be reckoned among its good or its bad consequences? Upon this point opinions differed. Mandeville's constant effort to play the ironist and *épater le bourgeois* makes his utterances on this as on most subjects equivocal. He affects, on one side, agreement with the traditional view; pride is an "odious Vice." But on the other side, its results—and this one in particular—*are* "public benefits." These benfits are enjoyed (he thinks) by the poor as well as the rich, since in a wealthy community more labor can be employed, and an increasing population can be supported. To produce his effect of paradox, Mandeville must constantly balance one side against the other. But it seems fairly clear that his chief concern was to emphasize the public benefits; and it is at least doubtful whether he would really have admitted that any human propensity of which the consequences are beneficial can be called a

[27] *The Love of Fame,* 1728, Sat. V, pp. 91, 55.

vice. The more conventional view was that expressed in the
lines of Young last quoted; *this* result of the "universal passion" is an evil, because men are happier when their wants
are few. To multiply desires is to multiply dissatisfactions;
and a desire which is by its very nature insatiable is worst
of all. This view was, of course, supported by the whole
primitivistic tradition coming down from classical antiquity,
and was obviously more in keeping with the Christian ethics.
And no one who regarded equality of conditions as a social
desideratum could regard as anything but evil a passion
which, because emulative, made for inequality.

Speaking of articles of luxury, Rousseau writes in *Émile,*
"Since the value of these useless products lies only in
l'opinion [*i. e.,* in their relation to men's appraisals of one
another], their price is itself a part of their value, and they
are esteemed in proportion as they are costly. The importance which the rich man attaches to them is not due to
their utility, but to the fact that the poor man cannot pay
for them." And Rousseau concludes with a Latin tag from
Petronius: *Nolo habere bona nisi quibus populus inviderit:*
"I don't want to have any goods except those that the pop-
ulace will envy me for possessing." But eighteenth-century
readers were not made familiar with the conception set
forth by Veblen in the twentieth merely by such *obiter dicta*
of religious moralists, embittered misanthropes, and satirical poets. It had been fully and emphatically expressed by
the founder of the science of political economy—not, indeed,
in *The Wealth of Nations,* but in the later editions of *The
Theory of Moral Sentiments.* It is chiefly from our "regard
to the sentiments of mankind," said Adam Smith, "that we

pursue riches and avoid poverty." By the "sentiments of
mankind" here Smith plainly means the ways in which those
with whom we associate think and feel about us. "For," he
continues,

> to what purpose is all the toil and bustle of this world?
> What is the end of avarice and ambition, of the pursuit of
> wealth, of power and pre-eminence? It is to supply the
> necessities of nature? The wages of the meanest labourer
> can supply them. . . . What then is the cause of our aver-
> sion to his situation? From whence, then, arises that em-
> ulation which runs through all the different ranks of men,
> and what are the advantages of that great purpose of
> human life which we call bettering our condition? To
> be observed, to be attended to, to be taken notice of with
> sympathy, complacency and approbation, are all the ad-
> vantages which we can propose to derive from it. It is the
> vanity, not the ease or the pleasure, which interests us.
> But vanity is always founded upon our belief of our being
> the object of attention and approbation. The rich man
> glories in his riches, because he feels that they naturally
> draw upon him the attention of the world. . . . At the
> thoughts of this, his heart seems to swell and dilate itself
> within him, and he is fonder of his wealth upon this
> account than for all the other advantages it procures him.
> The poor man, on the contrary, is ashamed of his poverty.
> He feels that it either places him out of sight of mankind,
> or that, if they take any notice of him, they have, how-
> ever, scarcely any fellow-feeling with the misery and dis-
> tress which he suffers. He is mortified and distressed
> upon both accounts; for though to be overlooked and to
> be disapproved of, are things entirely different, yet as

obscurity covers us from the daylight of honour and approbation, to feel that we are taken no notice of, necessarily damps the most agreeable hope, and disappoints the most ardent desire of human nature.[28]

It is evident from this passage, then, that Smith had in the eighteenth century enunciated the thesis which Veblen was to propound in the twentieth—a thesis which has often been acclaimed in the latter period as an original and notable contribution to economic theory. The founder of the science, or would-be science, of "Oeconomics" also held that the "consumption of goods cannot be said to afford the incentive from which accumulation invariably"—or ever—"proceeds"; that "the motive which lies at the root of ownership is emulation," the feeling that "the possession of wealth confers honour"; and that there is "no other conceivable incentive to the accumulation of wealth."

[28] *Theory of Moral Sentiments*, 6th edition (1790), Part I, Sec. III, Ch. 2.

Lecture VII

THE INDICTMENT OF PRIDE

In an earlier lecture I observed that there ran through the seventeenth and eighteenth centuries a long discussion over the question whether "pride," admittedly a universal and exceedingly potent passion in man, has chiefly benign or chiefly harmful consequences in individual and social life. At the one extreme was the opinion that it is the principal, or even the only, effective psychic source of all that is most needful and most desirable in human behavior whatever its intrinsic nature; at the other extreme was the opinion that it is the principal psychic source of most of the evils and miseries in man's existence. Between the extremes, there are to be found, of course, various intermediate views, in which some of the effects of this motive were regarded as good and some as bad. There were two distinct questions involved in the discussion: first, what *are* the modes of conduct, or the social phenomena, which are explicable, and explicable only, as consequences of the operation of this motive and would not exist without it; and second, what modes of conduct, or what features of the life of civilized society, are desirable and what undesirable. There could be, and were, differing opinions on both questions; or there might be agreement on the first and disagreement on the second. Two writers might attribute the *same* effects to "pride," but one of them might regard some or all of these effects as good, the other might consider them pernicious. The discussion was further complicated by the fact that—as has already been pointed out—it really had to do with the appraisal of more than one "passion" or type of motive, though the same name was often applied to these—approbativeness, self-esteem, and emulation, the craving for "distinction" or superiority. This last, it would appear, was usually regarded as a special form or derivative either of approbativeness or of the desire for self-esteem, or of both; the tendency to confuse them is not surprising, since, though they are analytically distinguishable, they tend in practice to shade off or pass over into one another. Self-esteem tends to lean heavily upon the assurance of the approval of others, and conversely, that assurance begets self-esteem; and the desires both for self-esteem and for approbation tend to assume the comparative or emulative form.

Our review of this discussion began with the favorable appraisal of "pride," in terms of its consequences. This, we saw, rested mainly on two premises, one relating to emulation, the other (and more frequently emphasized) to approbativeness. First, "pride," in the sense of the desire of individuals to gain esteem or distinction by surpassing the achievements of others, is the psychological cause of the progress of the species. Second, "pride," in the sense of the desire to be approved or admired by others, though it is undeniably a nonrational and a self-regarding desire, nevertheless, by its very nature, leads the individual to act as other individuals, or the community in general, desire him to act—in other words, to subordinate his private desires and interests to the public interest. It is, in fact, the principal, or the only dependable, motive for the behavior which is generally described as moral. If it is not a virtue, its overt effects are, in the main, the same as those of virtue; and it is far more potent.

The specific counts in the indictment of "pride," in terms of its concrete effects, were numerous and formidable. Emulative pride—and pride always, it was assumed, tends to be emulative—was declared, by one or another of those who inveighed against it, to be solely or chiefly responsible for the following evils with which human life is afflicted:

1. A multitude of desires for objects which are not needful for man's happiness, which, indeed, he would be far happier and better without.

2. Science and philosophy.

3. Unnatural excess of morality.

4. Inequality of various kinds, especially economic inequalities.

5. The demand for equality.

6. Most of the rivalries, jealousies, and conflicts between individuals and between classes within a society.

7. International wars.

8. The pursuit of insubstantial, purely imaginary values.

9. Insincerities and affectations which vitiate the inner integrity and the social intercourse of men.

10. What may be called hedonic parasitism, i.e., the obliteration of the very personality of the individual.

There is not time to examine the arguments advanced on each of these counts; I shall have to confine myself to two or three of them. The first of these charges was connected on the one hand with the theory concerning the motivation

of the acquisition of wealth with which I dealt in Lecture VI
—the theory which Veblen was to revive and elaborate in a
later age, and on the other hand with both the primitivistic
and the Christian traditions. Man in this world has certain
"real" or primary needs; "nature" has implanted in his
constitution desires which demand satisfaction. But these
are few and easily satisfied. A thousand moralists, ancient
and modern, had declared that the secret of happiness lies in
not wanting things, in restricting one's desires to the irreducible minimum, since the multiplication of desires is
simply the multiplication of dissatisfactions. The only fairly
sure way to be happy is to keep down the number of things
you cannot be happy without, as most of the ancient sages
had agreed. But men, or the vast majority of men, never
limit their desires to their needs; there is, indeed, no deter-
minate sum of goods which mankind, in the mass, ever
regards as sufficient. It is a species—the only species—of
animal which, however much it may have, always wants
more and therefore forever adds contrivance to contrivance,
possession to possession, luxury to luxury. And for this inter-
minable cumulativeness of human desires, there can, it was
argued, be only one explanation: pride. Beyond what is
requisite to satisfy the natural desire for comfort and ease,
things are desired, not for the enjoyment obtainable through
their use, but for the invidious distinction attaching to their
possession, as Mandeville showed. Young again sums up
the point, in lines not among his best:

A *decent competence* we fully taste;
It strikes our *sense*, and gives a constant feast:

More, we perceive by dint of *thought* alone;
The rich must *labour* to possess their *own,*
To feel their great abundance; and request
Their humble friends to *help* them to be *blest,*
To *see* their treasures, *hear* their glory told,
And *aid* the wretched *impotence* of gold.

To Burke, apparently to Mandeville, to Voltaire in one of his moods, and to many others, this effect of pride seemed a good thing; it meant progress not only in wealth but in the refinements of life, in inventions which increase man's power over nature, in the sciences and the arts. But to those who believed the simple life the best, who saw in this so-called progress only an increase in the laboriousness and complexity of existence and in the dependence of man's inner satisfactions upon outward things, the effect necessarily appeared wholly evil; and "pride" stood condemned as the source of it all.

This first reason for inveighing against pride was closely related to the second. As men are led by that passion to multiply material goods beyond the limits of necessity and real utility, so are they led by it to seek to increase knowledge beyond those limits. Is man either happier or morally better for knowing so much? If men of science and philosophers were not actuated by vanity, by the desire for esteem and distinction, if they sought only their own happiness and peace of mind and that of other men, would they conceivably engage in their arduous and tormenting labors, and all to gain a little sum of useless information about matters which it does not particularly behoove man to know? And *how* small and how dubious a sum! added the philosophical skeptic, at this point in the argument; how narrow the limits of the knowledge attainable by our weak faculties, and how shaky and uncertain the little that we fancy we have gained—as is shown by the perpetual disagreements among scholars and philosophers themselves. Some slight additions to man's physical comfort and convenience might perhaps be credited to past investigators of purely practical matters—though in the seventeenth and eighteenth centuries, before the more sensational achievements of modern technology and medicine which were to come, these contributions of science to the improvement of man's estate could hardly have seemed very impressive. And, it was argued, even such contributions were for the most part merely offsets to evils resulting from the increase in luxury and in the complexity of life which science had made possible. It was asked, with no doubt about the answer, were not savages healthier than civilized men, with all their doctors? As for what were called purely speculative inquiries, theoretical science as well as philosophy, their only results were conflicts of opinion, confusions of thought, and the diversion of men's minds from the rational pursuit of happiness.

This anti-intellectualist, antiscientific strain was no oddity of Rousseau's; it too was the continuation of an old tradition—or rather, of several old traditions. It had been conspicuous in the primitivism of classical antiquity, especially is Stoicism; Seneca was one of the principal sources for these arguments in the modern writers, though the connection between science and pride had been less developed by him.[1] And Christian religious motives conspired with classical in-

[1] Cf. Lovejoy and Boas, *Primitivism . . . in Antiquity*, 1935, pp. 263-280.

fluences, with philosophic skepticism, and with simple utili-
tarian considerations, to lead to the same conclusion: the
vanity of philosophizing and of most scientific pursuits, and
the consequent perniciousness of the pride that generates
them. I need hardly recall the passage in *Paradise Lost*
(Book VIII) in which Milton puts into the mouth of no less
an authority than an archangel the disparagement and ridicule of the science of astronomy, on the ground that it serves
neither to improve man's condition in this world nor to fit
him better for the next. Abbadie continues the strain in the
1690's, with the special emphasis upon the rôle of pride in
the matter which is pertinent to our theme:

> I ask you, of what profit is the greater part of those things
> in which we instruct a man who is made for Eternity?
> What do human sciences teach us?—words, etymologies,
> dates, facts which do not concern us or which serve only
> to show that we know them; vain or ridiculous or danger-
> ous questions, speculations without end, an infinity of fic-
> tions and falsehoods—and almost nothing that is useful to
> us, and that can give nourishment to our soul. The pursuit
> of all these things by learned men can be explained only
> on the supposition that *la vanité soit venue au secours de
> la science.* For it is an error to imagine that our minds
> love truth as such (*en tant que verité*). There are no
> truths greater or more important than those that every-
> body knows; yet there are none about which we are more
> indifferent. Why is this so? It is because truth does not
> seem to us desirable (*aymable*) for itself, but only in so
> far as *elle peut nous distinguer.*[2]

Without the religious note, the same derivation of specu-

[2] "The Art of Knowing One-Self," p. 469.

lative inquires from pride may be found in Voltaire. Though himself a *philosophe* of a sort, he thought emulative self-esteem the principal cause of the lucubrations of philosophers, or at any rate of the multiplicity of their systems, and the term "philosophers," it is to be remembered, then included scientific theorists:

> An ingenious and bold hypothesis, which has at first sight some glimmer of probability, solicits human pride to believe it; the mind finds ground for self-applause in the possession of principles of so subtle a kind, and makes use of all its ingenuity to defend them.[3]

Rousseau's passionate voicing of this anti-intellectualist note in the second *Discours de Dijon* is too familiar to need citation; but it is pertinent to our present topic to recall that if he there represents all the evils of civilized life—luxury, physical deterioration, the loss of man's original freedom and equality, the insincerities of polite society, the moral corruption of all classes—as consequences of the progress of the arts and sciences, he finds the ultimate psychic source of all of these in turn in pride. Each science and art had, it is true, its beginning in a different, though equally depraved, motive: "astronomy was born of superstition; eloquence, of ambition, hatred, flattery, mendacity; geometry, of avarice; physical science, of vain curiosity;" but *"toutes, et la morale même, de l'orgueil humain."* (The inclusion of "morals" here, rather unhappily for Rousseau's argument, among the progeny of pride, seems an inopportune reminiscence of Mandeville.) All the ills from which we

[3] *Traité de Metaphysique*, ch. III.

suffer are, then, "the punishment of the *efforts orgueilleux,* the efforts, due to pride, which we have made to transcend the happy ignorance in which the Eternal Wisdom had placed us."

The essay it is to be remembered, *did* win for Rousseau the prize in the competition in which it was entered; the Academicians of Dijon cannot, therefore, have considered his theses too strange and too contrary to all respectable precedent to deserve consideration. But the *Discourse* certainly shocked many of his contemporaries; for by the 1750's—and, indeed, a good deal earlier—the disparagement of science, and of the intellectual ambitions which give rise to it, ran counter to the dominant temper of the age. Rousseau, nevertheless, replying to his critics in the preface to his comedy *Narcisse* (1753), does not retreat from his so-called paradox, but heightens it and brings new arguments to its support. Explaining the meaning of his *First Discourse,* Rousseau declares that the "moral decline of all peoples in proportion as the taste for study and for letters is diffused among them" is not a mere coincidence, but the consequence of a *liaison nécessaire.* "For this taste can arise among a people only from two evil forces, which it in turn sustains and augments: *viz.,* indolence, and the desire to distinguish oneself." The science and art begotten of the latter desire produce "evils infinitely more dangerous than all the goods to which it gives rise are useful: it ends by rendering those who are inspired by this desire all too little scrupulous about the means of attaining success." For the itch for literary or philosophical distinction, Rousseau observes, with some justice—and with greater pertinency to

a later age than to his own—inevitably tends to make it
seem more important to be original than to be right.

> The first philosophers gained a great reputation by teach-
> ing men the practice of their duties and the principles of
> virtue. But soon, these principles having grown common,
> it became necessary to distinguish oneself by striking out
> contrary routes. Such is the origin of the absurd systems
> of Leucippus, of Diogenes, of Pyrrho, of Protagoras, of
> Lucretius, Hobbes and Mandeville, and a thousand others
> among us have sought to distinguish themselves by similar
> means; and their dangerous doctrine has borne fruit to
> such an extent that one is terrified to see what point our
> Age of Reasoners has pushed in its maxims the contempt
> for the duties of man and of the citizen. . . . A taste for
> philosophy weakens all the bonds of esteem and mutual
> good will which attach men to society; this, perhaps, is
> the most dangerous of the evils which it engenders. . . .
> By force of observing men and reflecting upon humanity,
> the philosopher learns to appreciate them at their true
> value; and it is difficult to have a great deal of affection
> for what one despises. Presently he focusses upon himself
> all the interests which men of virtue share with their
> fellows; his contempt for others turns to the profit of his
> own pride; his *amour-propre* grows in the same propor-
> tion as his indifference for the rest of the world.

What, incidentally, is piquant here is Rousseau's betrayal
of the contradictory leanings of his own thought. Philosophy, he assumes, leads to a low opinion of mankind, and
this, he implies, is a just opinion. His own appraisal of
human nature as it actually is—that is, since *l'amour-propre*
has become dominant in it—is an eminently unfavorable

one; and history, which is the spectacle of human nature in action, is to him (in one of his moods) a long, sad story of follies, miseries, and crimes. Though he sometimes dwells on the natural goodness of man, he could not consistently believe in it. For if pride is an evil motive, and is also the most pervasive and powerful motive, it follows that the nature of man is morally evil; what is clearest about man is his *méchanceté naturelle.* Philosophy, itself the offspring of this now universal passion, leads to this "true appreciation" of man, to the view which Rousseau, in his more consistent moments, accepted. But this view is mischievous to society; therefore it ought not to be held; therefore philosophers, who, he thinks, are likely to hold it, ought to be abolished!

These two tendencies of thought, which provided arguments for the indictment of pride, remained, it need hardly be said, almost wholly without effect, outside of the printed page. While they were still widely manifest in literature and philosophy, scarcely anyone's practice was influenced by them. A Boswell might occasionally yearn to go and live with the savages, a Chateaubriand might actually do so for a time, with disillusioning results. But natural science, whatever its motivation, went on its way untroubled by the attacks upon it; technology continued to bring forth many devices making the life of, at least, the prosperous classes more luxurious, more complicated, and more cumbered with apparatus; and the philosophers continued to multiply systems disagreeing with one another, if possible, more extensively than before. If "pride" was the chief cause of all these things, then pride proved itself too stubborn and ubiquitous an element in human nature to be extirpated, or even sensibly weakened, by the preachments of either the Christian or the primitivistic moralists.

We come now to the last, which is also the subtlest and, on its face, the gravest, count in the indictment. It is one of those directed, not against what might be held to be the potentially corrigible aberrations or excesses of pride— the exaggerations of self-esteem, or the emulative form either of that passion or of approbativeness—but against approbativeness as such, that is, against that one among the three desires classed under the name of "pride" which to many seemed the most amiable and most benign—the desire for the approval, esteem, regard, or admiration of one's fellows, the "love of fame." By this, as by a deep-seated canker, it was argued long before Rousseau, the very inner life of the individual may be, and tends to be, eaten out. In so far as it has taken possession of a man, he no longer has, so to say, a mind or heart of his own; he subsists upon other men's opinions, upon their praise or blame, or rather, upon his often deceptive fancy about their opinions of him. He ceases to exist in and for himself; the substance of his being has been converted into a more or less illusory image in his own mind of an image of him in other minds; and the standards by which he appraises even this image are not his own standards but theirs.

The thought had long since been concisely expressed by Lucretius, in his description of the type of men who aspire to be *clari et potentes* (famous and powerful) and therefore push into "the narrow pathway of ambition"; these, he says,

Sapiunt ex ore alieno, petuntque
Res ex auditis potius quam sensibus ipsis:

"they get the taste of things from other men's mouths, and pursue objects because of what they have heard others say, rather than because of what their own senses tell them."[4]

Some of the later expressions of the thought may be echoes or elaborations of this Lucretian theme. In the seventeenth century Pascal's is, so far as I know, the most penetrating statement of this conception of approbativeness as a kind of living-at-second-hand.

We are not content with the life we have in ourselves and with our own existence; we wish to live an imaginary life in the thought of others, and we consequently force ourselves to *appear*. We labor incessantly to embellish and preserve our imaginary being, and neglect the real one. And if we have tranquillity of mind or generosity or loyalty, we try to have it known, in order to attach these virtues to our *other*, imaginary being; and we would be willing to detach them from ourselves in order to attach them to the other. We should cheerfully be cowards in order to get the reputation of being brave.[5]

La Placette's indictment of pride on this ground is comparable to Pascal's, but was perhaps borrowed from it.

Everyone conceives of what others think of him as a second existence which he has in the public mind, the

---

[4] *De rerum natura*, VI, 1134-5. The English translators of Lucretius (Munro, Rouse, Leonard) have missed the point of these lines. See *Primitivism . . . in Antiquity*, 1935, p. 233, *n.* 16.

[5] *Pensées*, ed. Giraud, No. 147.

good and evil of which belong to him no less than the good and evil of the real and veritable being which he has in himself. Everyone is greatly occupied with adding all possible perfections to this second being; and this is the immediate object of all that we do to please [others] and to make ourselves esteemed. It is this that makes us so much love praise and manifestations of respect, as so many proofs of the perfection and the happiness of this imaginary being outside of us.[6]

Boileau, limited, perhaps, by the exigencies of rhymed verse, expresses the thought less subtly than these prose writers, but goes even farther than they by declaring approbativeness to be the source of *all* our woes:

C'est là de tous nos maux le fatal fondement:
Des jugemens d'autrui nous tremblons follement:
Et chacun l'un de l'autre adorant les caprices,
Nous cherchons hors de nous nos vertus et nos vices.
Misérables jouets de notre vanité,
Faisons au moins l'aveu de notre infirmité.[7]

But Boileau in the end admits that one is not cured of this malady by becoming conscious of it and of its absurdity and its unhappy consequences; he concludes the *Epistel to Arnauld* from which the lines are taken:

Et, même sur ces vers que je te viens d'écrire,
Je tremble en ce moment de ce que l'on va dire.

Rousseau, finally, in the *Second Discourse*, probably borrowing from these precursors, makes this idea concerning

[6] *Traité de l'orgueil*, p. 52.
[7] *Épitre* III, 17-20.

approbativeness the climax of his comparison between the savage and the civilized man.[8] He imagines a Carib Indian visiting Europe (*this*, incidentally, was a borrowing from Montaigne) and observing

the painful and envied labors of a minister of state. How many cruel deaths would not this indolent savage prefer to the horror of such a life, which often is not even rendered more endurable by the pleasure of doing good! But, in order to understand the object of all this toil, it is necessary that these words, *power* and *reputation*, should have a meaning to the savage's mind; that he should learn that there exists a kind of men who *comptent pour quelque chose les regards du reste de l'univers*, who look upon the thoughts of the rest of the world about them as a thing of some consequence—men who are able to be happy and content with themselves upon the testimony of others rather than their own. Such is, in fact, the true cause of all these differences [between the savage and civilized man]: the savage lives in himself, *l'homme sociable*, the socialized man, always outside of himself. He is capable of living only in the opinion of others, and it is, so to say, solely from their judgment that he draws the feeling of his own existence.

Rousseau, it need hardly be said, derived his conceptions of the savage character largely from the primitivistic tradition and partly from his own imagination, though he had read the *Histoire des voyages*, and, recognizing that little careful and competent factual study of the life of primitive

[8] It is of some interest to note that Boileau and Rousseau held precisely the same view concerning the source of all our evils.

peoples had been made, he was one of the earliest prophets of the science of ethnology.⁹ But if he had himself lived among savages, he would have found them enduring, when tribal custom required, tortures considerably more strange and *pénibles* than those of a European minister of state; and he would perhaps have discovered much reason for suspecting that in this they are actuated by the same motives—a fear of tribal reprobation and a *fureur de se distinguér*. If he had made this discovery, he would have been unable to regard even the savages as exempt from this strange tendency to transfer *hors de soi,* to the picture of oneself in one's fellows' thoughts, the values which one seeks to realize. It would then have appeared to him a universal human characteristic.

And in fact, in the Preface to *Narcisse,* with a glaring but apparently unconscious inconsistency, he ascribes to the savages precisely the opposite characteristic to that attributed to them in the *Second Discourse*: they *do* consider "the thoughts of the rest of the world about them a thing of some consequence"; their moral superiority, indeed, consists in an extreme degree of approbativeness.

⁹ In *Discours sur l'origine de l'inégalité,* note 7. See my *Essays in the History of Ideas,* "The Supposed Primitivism of Rousseau's *Discourse on Inequality.*" Rousseau, as this essay points out, was not a chronological primitivist; he did not regard the "state of nature," in the sense of the original condition of mankind, as the ideal state; nor was he a thorough-going cultural primitivist. But he did regard the life of savages in the patriarchal and pastoral stage of the development of culture as better than any of the later stages—though itself by no means ideal. In this sense, and in this sense only, he may be called a "primitivist."

For, he assures us, among savages, "public esteem is the *only* good to which each of them aspires, and which they all of them merit."[10] In short, *le bon sauvage* lives "outside of himself" *more* than civilized man does. Nevertheless in *Émile* Rousseau continues to represent this propensity as the final and consummatory stage of the mental abberrations of mankind:

> From the womb of so many diverse passions I perceive opinion [i.e., the opinions of others about oneself] mounting upon an unshakable throne, and stupid mortals, enslaved to its empire, basing their own existence exclusively upon the judgments of others.[11]

This count in the indictment of approbativeness, it will be observed, precisely reversed the usual argument for the beneficial effect of the operation of this element in human nature. According to that argument, as we have seen, the craving for esteem, or the "love of fame," was held to be a fortunate propensity of man just because it substitutes, *within* the individual, for his naturally partial judgments of himself and his self-seeking desires, the relatively disinterested and impartial judgments and the desires of other individuals or of the community to which he belongs. It was an ingenious device of the Creator by which men—in so far as this motive was effective in them—were, so to say, emancipated from the egocentric predicament in their valuations of ends and their appraisals of themselves. But just this substitution of others' valuations and appraisals for one's own is now declared to be an intrinsically evil thing, and

[10] *Oeuvres*, 1865, V, p. 107.   [11] *Oeuvres*, 1865 ed., II, p. 185.

approbativeness, therefore, to be the most deplorable of all man's follies.

But some of those, e.g., Pascal, who decried or deplored approbativeness were not chiefly considering whether it is indispensable for the good order of society or for the evocation of human energies which would otherwise be exercised feebly or not at all. Certain of them manifestly felt a sort of repugnance at the very idea of this attitude; it seemed to them a thing intrinsically bad, whatever its results on men's overt behavior. It is worth while, I think, to try to discern *why* they felt so, to observe or conjecture the underlying grounds or causes of this disapprobation of approbativeness as such.

A. In part it seems to have been a species of quasi-aesthetic dislike of the spectacle which this human trait presented —the spectacle of the individual living and acting, not from inner sources of his own, not as a self-contained entity, but as a kind of parasite upon the thought of him entertained by other mortals, and upon *their* valuations. This could not, indeed, without absurdity, be supposed to be universally and completely true of men, though some who wrote in this vein seemed to imply that it could. A universal and complete mutual parasitism would be a contradiction in terms; it would be like a universe consisting wholly of mirrors, with nothing to be reflected in them. But the standards and valuations by which men judge one another could not all be second-hand. *Somebody* must have originated them in the first place. But the suggestion that such a situation was possible may be regarded as a rhetorical exaggeration, not to be taken seriously. For those who were

revolted by approbativeness as such, the point was that that
propensity made the individual dependent upon other men
both for his judgments and his sources of self-satisfaction;
and this was felt to be a humiliating and reprehensible condition for a human being to live in.

B. Yet this very feeling, evidently, arose in part from another kind of pride. It was a revulsion of self-esteem *against*
approbativeness. To conceive of ourselves as thus dependent
upon others, and of our actions as subservient to their praise
or blame, is not flattering to our *amour-propre*. There is an
element of humility in approbativeness; it is an implicit
recognition of the limitation of our own competence as
judges of values and of ourselves. The proudest souls have
therefore always wished to think of themselves as immune
from it—though it is improbable that they ever have been
wholly immune.

C. Another ground for the adverse judgment of this attitude is evident in Boileau's lines already cited. The opinions of others before which we tremble, he implies, have no
rational validity. They are but the "caprices" of other mortals no less foolish than ourselves; why, then, should we be
concerned about them? Approbativeness—at least an approbativeness that is unselective, which it often is—is a ridiculous thing because it is self-contradictory. Abbadie observed
that we commonly wish for the approbation or admiration
even of those whom we despise. But if another man is an
object of contempt,

why should we be solicitous for his esteem; or if his
esteem is worthy of being the strongest passion of our

souls, how can we hold him in contempt? Is not our
scorn of our neighbor more affected than genuine? We
confusedly recognize his greatness, inasmuch as his
esteem appears to us of so great value; but we make every
effort to conceal our recognition of it from ourselves in
order to honor ourselves the more.[12]

D. There was, however, a deeper ground than any of these
for the feeling of an inherent moral evil in approbativeness.
It is evident in Pascal. He points to the undeniable fact that
the imaginary, the public self, to which we desire favorable
adjectives to attach in the minds of other men, need not
correspond to the real self. The desire of approbation is not
intrinsically and primarily a desire to *be,* but to appear. To
derive one's satisfaction simply from the pleasing image of
the public self is to be content with the appearance, the
phantasm, of virtue or excellence, without concern for the
qualities of the actual self without which there is no virtue
or excellence. To love your neighbor, that is, to desire his
happiness, is one thing; to love to think of yourself as loving
your neighbor is another thing; and to love to be thought
of as one who loves his neighbor is yet another thing.
Moral worth—so the reasoning runs—belongs only to the
first of these desires; the others, even though they may help
to cause you actually to make sacrifices for your neighbor's
happiness, are morally bad motives, because they are, at best,
substitutes for or diversions from the real thing, and at
worst falsifications. And men's universal consciousness of
this, numerous other writers remarked, is shown by the

[12] *L'art de se connnoistre soy-même,* p. 464.

fact that approbativeness always seeks to hide itself. Young writes, when declaiming on this side of the case,

> To shew the strength and infamy of pride,
> By all 'tis follow'd, and by all denied.
> What numbers are there, which at once pursue
> Praise, and the glory to contemn it, too!
> Vincenna knows self-praise betrays to shame,
> And therefore lays a stratagem for fame;
> Makes his approach in modesty's disguise
> To win applause, and takes it by surprise.
> 'To err,' says he, 'in small things is my fate.'
> You know your answer, 'He's exact in great.'
> 'My *style*,' says he 'is rude and full of faults.'
> 'But oh! what sense! what energy of thoughts.'[13]

Men said La Bruyère, wish in their hearts "to be esteemed, and they carefully conceal this desire, because they wish to pass for virtuous; and to wish to obtain from virtue any advantage other than virtue itself—that is to say, to obtain esteem and praise—would *not* be to be virtuous, but to love esteem and praise—in other words, to be vain. Men are very vain, and they hate nothing so much as to be regarded as vain."[14]

Now, that there is much truth in these last reflections upon approbativeness is not open to question. It is a desire which can be satisfied with the appearance of merit rather than the reality; and it is the trait in human nature which makes possible many of the subjective states and attitudes in men

---

[13] *The Love of Fame;* in Young, *Works*, 1767, I, p. 105.

[14] *Les Charactères: De l'homme* (1696), 1, 24.

which all men most dislike—which, in short, are generally
disapproved. It makes them possible, but not necessary; and
even upon this last count, therefore, the indictment cannot
be fully sustained; no general condemnation of this element
in our affective make-up follows from the facts about it
which Pascal and the rest have pointed out. It would in any
case, of course, be a futile and silly thing to pronounce a
general condemnation upon a human characteristic which is
universal and inexpugnable.

One therefore cannot but wonder what practical result the
denouncers of pride hoped to accomplish. One might lament
the existence in man of the passions going under that name,
but if—as many who decried them held—they constituted
the psychic differentiae of the species, one could hardly expect to eliminate them. Numerous writers, nevertheless, had
the air of seeking to eliminate them by dilating upon both
their intrinsic absurdities and their unhappy consequences.
There were others who seem to have sometimes believed it
possible and needful for men to free themselves from these
passions and therefore exhorted them to do so; yet at other
times they became mindful both of the enormous difficulty, if
not the absolute impossibility, of extirpating pride and
shame from the human mind, and also of their value to
society—and therefore in the end gave them a place among
the permissible springs of action. Spinoza, I think, must
classed among these waverers—these perhaps judicious
waverers. "Glory and shame," he writes in the *Short Treatise*,[15] "are not only of no advantage, . . . but they are perni-

[15] "Glory" is defined by Spinoza as "pleasure associated with
the idea of some action of our own which we imagine to be

cious and must be rejected." They are to be rejected not only for practical but for metaphysical reasons. For they "by their definitions" presuppose praise and blame—or praiseworthiness and blameworthiness; and praise and blame (Spinoza assumes) presuppose the freedom of the will, which is for him an illusion. We should never praise or blame one another's actions if we realized that they are not "caused" by ourselves as separate individuals, but by the necessary implications of the eternally necessary attributes of God or Substance. Spinoza sometimes, it is true, applies the logic of his determinism only to shame, and not to pride; a man may legitimately be pleased with himself, and accept credit for his virtue, if his conduct is in fact good, but it is irrational of him to feel remorse if his conduct is evil, for "he may rest assured that it was necessary and unavoidable."[16] But this distinction seems inconsistent with Spinoza's doctrine as a whole which implies that a man's good and bad deeds are equally inevitable; if blame for the bad is irrational, so is praise for the good.

Meanwhile, lest I leave an erroneous conception of the position of Pascal on the question with which this lecture has been concerned, I must add that he does *not* in the end conclude that man's approbativeness is merely a thing to be deplored or condemned. For such a mind as his it was hardly

---

praised by others," "shame" (*pudor*) as "grief associated with the idea of some action of our own which we imagine to be blamed or ill spoken of (*oituperari*) by others."

[16] Cf. David A. Bidney's illuminating exposition of these points, *The Ethics and Psychology of Spinoza*, pp. 208-9, 321-2, 328.

possible to adopt either simple alternative—that this passion of glory is essentially an evil or that it is essentially a good; he must show it to be both. For his constant aim, as he himself tells us, when writing of human nature, was both to lower and to raise man in his own eyes; and he finds means of doing both at once in this one attribute of approbativeness. "The *recherche de la gloire* is the basest thing in man (*la plus grande bassesse*) ; but it is just this which is also the greatest mark of his excellence." For, Pascal thinks, this craving is a sort of involuntary and irrepressible recognition both of the authority of reason and of its presence in some degree in other men; and it is also the unconscious disclosure of a desire to conform to it oneself.

> [Men] rate so high the reason of man, that, whatever advantages they may have on the earth, they are not content unless they also have a favorable position in man's *reason. C'est la plus belle place du monde.* . . . Even those who despise men and place them on the same level as the brutes, still wish to be admired and beloved by them; and they contradict themselves by virtue of their own feeling (*sentiment,* i.e., the desire for esteem)—their *nature*, which is stronger than anything else, convincing them more powerfully of the greatness of man than their reason convinces them of their baseness.[17]

Nothing could be more Pascalesque than the ingenious and seemingly contradictory involution of the thought here: approbativeness is an ignoble and irrational desire; it is, nevertheless, an implicit appeal to reason, on the part of those who

[17] *Pensées*, ed. Giraud, No. 404; italics mine.

feel it; as such, it is the crowning evidence of a fundamental rationality in themselves and in all men; and it therefore confutes the reason itself which declares it to be ignoble and irrational! But what, behind the paradoxicality of his way of putting things, Pascal was evidently asserting was that to seek approbation implies the recognition of the existence of some publicly valid, impersonal standard of the approvable —of which the judgment of other men, or of the generality of men, is (even though often mistakenly) taken as the expression.

The assumption of the intrinsic evil of pride as a motive of human behavior presented especial difficulties for those who theorized about the education of the young. William Law, in this respect, was a precursor of Rousseau. In a chapter of his *Serious Call* Law is discussing the method of moral education. If anything was to be *done* about "pride," if the evils said to result from it were to be stopped at the source, it was obviously necessary to prevent this emotion and desire from arising in the mind during the formative period of childhood, or if it could not be prevented altogether, to repress it as much as possible. But the actual practice in education was, as Mandeville had pointed out, not to repress but to intensify this passion; it was found to be the most effective motive to which to appeal in training the child to conform to the standards of behavior desired and approved by the social group; and, according to Mandeville, that result could be attained in no other way. Law agrees with Mandeville as to the actual practice of parents and teachers of their time; but *he* sees in just this feature of "our modern education" the prime cause of the disorders of society.

> The first temper that we try to awake in children is pride;
> . . . we stir them up to action from principles of strife and
> ambition, from *glory, envy,* and a desire of distinction,
> that they may excel others, and shine in the eyes of the
> world. . . . And when we have taught them to scorn to be
> outdone by any, to hear no *rival,* to thirst after *every in-
> stance* of applause, to be content with nothing but the
> highest distinctions; then we begin to take comfort in
> them, and promise the world some mighty things from
> youths of such glorious spirit.[18]
>
> That this is the nature of our *best education* is too plain
> to need any proof. . . . And after all this, we complain of
> the effects of pride; we wonder to see *grown men* acted
> and governed by ambition, envy, *scorn,* and a desire of
> glory; not considering that they were all the time of their
> youth called upon to [base] all their action and industry
> upon the same principles. You teach a child to *scorn* to
> be outdone, to thirst for *distinction* and *applause;* and
> is it any wonder that he continues to act all his life in the
> same manner?[19]

The consequences of this sort of education are evil because,
Law (with dubious truth) argues, so-called "emulation" is,
at best, "nothing else but a *refinement* upon envy, or rather
the most *plausible* part of that . . . passion. . . . For *envy* is
not an *original* temper, but the natural, necessary and unavoidable effect of emulation, or a desire of glory; and there
is no other possible way of destroying emulation, or a desire
of glory." And envy is an emotion evil in itself, and produc-

[18] *Serious Call* (1729) in *Works,* 1892-3, IV, p. 182.
[19] *Ibid.,* p. 183.

tive only of discord and antisocial behavior. The model father, then, who is introduced to sum up Law's educational ideas, exhorts his son:

Above all, mark this, never do anything through strife, or envy, or emulation or vainglory. Never do anything in order to excel other people, but in order to please God, and because it is his will that you should do everything in the best manner that you can. . . . Hate and despise all *human* glory, for it is nothing else but human folly. It is the greatest *snare*, and the greatest *betrayer*, that you can possibly admit to your heart.

Nearly all of this might appropriately have found a place in the Second or Third Book of Rousseau's *Émile*, which dealt with preadolescent education. This species of passions —pride and vanity—Rousseau opined, "do not have their germ in the heart of the child, and cannot arise in it of themselves. It is we who introduce them into it, and it is only through our fault that they ever take root there." Émile's tutor, accordingly, avoids even suggesting the possibility of such a motive, so long as his pupil is a child. But it is otherwise, Rousseau finds, with the heart of the adolescent; "whatever we may do, these passions will arise in it in spite of us;" and it is for this reason that the problem of adolescent education is radically different from that of the education of children. When the youth first becomes interested in the other sex, he begins to desire also their admiration, and that of his fellows in general; he becomes intensely concerned about what others are thinking about him. This preoccupation naturally assumes the form of a comparison between himself and his like and generates a desire to be recognized as a superior kind of fellow. And so "emulation, rivalries, and jealousy" are born in him. Such, in brief, is Rousseau's account of the genesis of pride in the individual—and of all the evils which flow from it in society. But even though it originates spontaneously and inevitably at this stage of individual development, a prime object even in adolescent education must be to bring the youth to recognize and avoid its dangers.

There was a current—or a perennial—objection to the proposal to dispense with pride as a motive in education, namely (as Law puts it) that "ambition, and a desire of glory, are necessary to excite young people to industry; and that if we press upon them the duty of humility, we should deject their minds, and sink them into dulness and idleness." Law's reply to this, unfortunately, is indirect and evasive of the empirical question: *can* the maximal energy be excited, especially in the young, without appeal to the motivation which he wished to abolish? Pascal's principles also required him to deplore no less earnestly than Law any appeal to pride in education, and he had, in fact, done so much more briefly. But he had had an opportunity to see the experiment of eliminating that appeal tried at the famous school at Port Royal; and he was constrained to admit that it had been an unsuccessful experiment. "Admiration," he writes in one of the *Pensées*, spoils everything, beginning in childhood; [people say in the child's hearing] 'Oh, how well he speaks! Oh, how well he did that! What a good boy he is!' etc." Pascal immediately adds: "The children of Port Royal, to whom this spur of envy and glory is not applied, fall into listlessness, *tombent dans la nonchalance*."[20] If this bit of empirical evidence was typical, it seemed to follow that it is a dangerous error to make no use in education of motives so deeply rooted in human nature as self-esteem, approbativeness, and emulation. It was, perhaps, a special case of the common error of the perfectionist, who, feeling deeply that men *ought* to act only from the loftiest and most impersonal motives, has done a good deal of mischief in this imperfect world by proceeding on the assumption that human beings can be dealt with as if they *were* universally capable of habitually acting from such motives.

[20] *Pensées*, ed. Giraud, 151.

Lecture VIII 🐍 🐍 🐍

SOME ETHICAL REFLECTIONS

We shall be concerned in this lecture chiefly with certain aspects of the reflections on ethics of Hume and Adam Smith. There are, evidently, *two* classes of phenomena pertinent to morals that need to be analyzed; moral judgments, and the motivation of moral choices or acts. An account of the nature of the feelings or desires from which what is called moral behavior springs would not, of itself, clarify the nature or meaning of the judgments which men are constantly making as to what is to be considered good or bad, right or wrong, behavior. A purely contemplative angel, who himself never had anything to do except think, might still make judgments of this sort. We must, then, consider first the nature of the moral judgment and second the nature of the moral motive.

Now moral judgments are, or appear to be, propositions; and the question about a proposition is (except for some of our latter-day pragmatists) not what actions result from accepting it, but whether it is true or false; and the question whether a proposition is true or false would seem to fall within the domain of the understanding, not of the emotions or desires. None the less, moral judgments must obviously be somehow connected with moral motives; a set of propositions or reasonings in ethics which was declared to be true, but also declared to be incapable of affecting anybody's conduct, would be the most useless thing in the world; indeed, it would be hard to see what could be meant by calling it true, *as ethics*.

Hume's first problem, then—and, as he would hold, the problem of any ethical theorist—is to formulate a conception of the moral judgment which will make it intelligible that such a judgment can also be, or give rise to, a moral motive, a spring of action. And, in accordance with his central thesis, this can be done only if the moral judgment itself is, at least in part, the *expression* of an affective, or emotional, state or attitude of the person making the judgment, what I have earlier called a hedonic susceptibility. And this is, Hume maintains, the fact. When you examine what a moral judgment *means*, you find that it is primarily, if not exclusively, a proposition asserting, or rather, disclosing, the existence in the subject of a certain state of feeling, which can eventuate in a desire.

In considering this account of the moral judgment, it is to be borne in mind, in the first place, that moral judgments are for Hume (and for Adam Smith) exclusively judgments of approbation or disapprobation of persons or their motives, feelings, or purposes. They are concerned with what I have called adjectival, not with telic, values—with qualities manifested *in* action, not with ends to be attained *through* action. It is true that Hume in the end seeks to connect adjectival values with telic, or terminal, values; we approve, he finds, those *qualities* of persons which seem to us to have as their *effect* the realization of a certain kind of end; and this attempted synthesis of the two kinds of values is a distinctive feature of his doctrine, when considered in its entirety. Nevertheless, the moral judgment *as such* is never the evaluation of an end to be attained, but always the approbation (or disapprobation) of a personal quality, feeling, motive, or character; and though it *may* contain, so to say, a cross-reference to an end, it does not in fact always do so.

But what, specifically, is the feeling and desire of which a moral judgment is the expression? Hume observes, in substance, it is an obvious fact about us that we feel pleasure or pain not only in ourselves actually experiencing various states-of-things, but also in the *ideas* of states-of-things—in his own phraseology, in the "view or contemplation" of them. The relative *date* of the pleasure or pain must be noted here. The pleasure, or its opposite, occurs at the moment of "viewing" or "contemplating" whatever the thing is the idea of which is accompanied by pleasure. Hume himself does not make this point explicit and is, in fact, rather confused about it; but it is an obvious implication of his reasoning. And among the things of which the mere "view" gives us pleasure are certain kinds of action on the part of human beings or, more precisely, certain kinds of subjective qualities or characters in them which we infer from their actions. This is just an empirical fact about human nature, to be recognized as such; it does not need to be, and, indeed, cannot be, either explained or justified. We are, and, he thinks, cannot but be, pleased by the "spectacle" of actions which seem to us to manifest in those who perform them such qualities as generosity, magnanimity, benevolence, fortitude, self-control; we are displeased by the spectacle of actions which seem to manifest cruelty, treachery, meanness, cowardice, and weakness. And we love or hate, praise or blame, those qualities of which the contemplation "excites in us a satisfaction or uneasiness."

Now, in describing this type of affective reaction of ours to the ideas of certain kinds of human qualities, we have, Hume declares, already described the moral judgment. Approval and disapproval *are* these reactions and nothing more. We express these attitudes by saying that certain qualities or motives are virtuous, excellent, or admirable, or are vicious, evil, or contemptible; but what we mean by these adjectives is simply that the ideas of the qualities give rise in us to pleasant or unpleasant feelings, of varying degrees of intensity.

> An action, or sentiment, or character, is virtuous or vicious; why?; because its view causes a pleasure or uneasiness of a particular kind. . . . To have the sense of virtue is nothing but to *feel* a satisfaction of a particular kind from the contemplation of a character. The very *feeling constitutes* our praise or admiration.[1]

What, however, does Hume mean by speaking here, and elsewhere, of a "satisfaction" or "pleasure *of a particular kind*." In strictness, I take it, there are no differences of kind (as distinct from degree) among pleasures. There are, however, differences in the total complexes of content of consciousness of which pleasantness may be an ingredient. The pleasure may be associated with or conditioned by one or another sensation, image, or concept of a state-of-things. And by the "particular kind" of pleasure which distinguishes the moral judgment, what Hume apparently signifies is pleasure arising from the "view" of certain human qualities when these are

---

[1] *Treatise*, Bk. III, Pt. 1, Sec. 2; Selby-Bigge, ed., p. 471.

regarded disinterestedly, that is, in abstraction from their possible relation to any *future* satisfaction of our own, distinct from the present satisfaction which we have in contemplating them. For Hume points out that our judgments of approbation are neither identical with, nor inferred from, our judgments as to what *will* be to our advantage or disadvantage. " 'Tis only when a character is considered in general, without reference to our particular interest, that it causes such a feeling or sentiment as denominates it morally good or evil."

These characteristics which Hume considers the essentials of the moral judgment are evidently the same as those usually attributed to the aesthetic judgment; and Hume may be said to regard the former as a variety of the latter, differing from the other varieties in that it relates, not to external objects or works of art, but to subjective human qualities actually or potentially manifested in voluntary acts. For an aesthetic judgment also is, or has very frequently been described as, the expression of a present satisfaction arising directly from the "contemplation" of something, without conscious reference to any *future* advantage of the beholder. Hume and Smith, therefore, like their precursors Shaftesbury and Hutcheson, frequently speak of "moral taste," of an immediate sense of "moral beauty, deformity, or ugliness" inherent in the qualities or motives of persons.

There is, however, one conspicuous difference between moral judgment and ordinary aesthetic judgments which Hume implicitly recognizes but does not make sufficiently explicit. An aesthetic judgment is an enjoyment *in* the contemplation of a work of art, for example, and has no necessary reference to action to be performed. A moral judgment, even though disinterested in the sense that it is not concerned with the "*particular* interest" of the person making it, does usually have a reference to action to be performed. We may, it is true, simply enjoy contemplating the spectacle of, say, the "moral beauty" of the character of St. Francis; and our approbations or disapprobations of past acts or their motives are commonly of this *purely* contemplative sort. But obviously the more important instances of such judgments refer to future acts, or motives, of other men or of ourselves, to states-of-things not yet realized, which we wish to be realized; they are, in short, accompanied by desires, in the way previously defined. This fact is one which Hume might have been expected especially to emphasize since his chief concern is to describe the moral judgment in such a way that its power to affect action may be psychologically intelligible.

In spite of omissions in his account of such judgments, Hume, in insisting upon their quasi-aesthetic character, raises one of the fundamental issues of moral philosophy. His descriptive psychology of moral experience here brings sharply into view a question of ethics. It is the question whether what I have called adjectival values *are* genuine, independent, and irreducible values. Are the *qualities* of the *inner states* of human beings from which their actions arise valuable only as instrumental to ulterior ends, to consummatory satisfactions; or have they an undeterminative value, or disvalue, of their own? Doubtless generosity, benevolence, honesty, courage, and the like are useful to the agent or to others; but are they good only because of their utility, or good because of an excellence inherent in their very existence?

Hume's answer to this question (in this part of his doctrine) is evident from what has already been said; and I incline to think it is the right answer. If it is assumed that there are such things as aesthetic, noninstrumental values, there is no evident *a priori* reason why they should not be exemplified in the subjective qualities and characters of human agents, as well as in sensible objects; and it is certain, at least, as Hume declared, that our actual judgments or appraisals of the former are not usually recognitions simply of the instrumental value of these qualities, but assertions that they are themselves good or bad and are so even when, through force of circumstances, they are prevented from producing their external consequences. On the higher degrees of approbation or disapprobation—that is, admiration or contempt—this is especially evident. We admire or despise *persons* as agents, not the ends which their acts accomplish; and we admire them because of what they *are* (or are believed by us to be), what types of thoughts and feelings and attitudes are present in them, and what motives prompt their acts. An ethics which ignores this fact, which concerns itself with the nature of 'the good' and not also and primarily with the nature of goodness, misses the most conspicuous and distinctive characteristic of the moral judgments which men actually make.

But Hume's account of the moral judgment thus far seems to leave out another of its actual components. When people —or at all events most people—say 'Socrates was a good man,' or 'generosity is a virtue,' or 'it is wrong to oppress the helpless,' they do not in fact conceive themselves *merely* to be reporting upon the state of their own emotions. They are not, or do not appear to themselves to be, talking about themselves at all, but about Socrates, or generosity, or oppression of the helpless, and they are uttering what they suppose are true, or at least potentially true, propositions about the subjects to which these sentences relate. According to Hume's reasoning up to this point, the predicates of such propositions have no meaning except as designations of a pleasant or unpleasant feeling on the part of the person speaking; the predicates, in fact, all have the same meaning though expressed by different words, namely: 'something causing pleasure in me when contemplated.' That is to say: one of these sentences means 'the character of Socrates causes pleasure in me when I contemplate it'; another, 'the class of acts commonly called generous cause pleasure in me when I contemplate them'; and so on.

Now it may be true, and I think it is, that people in general would find it impossible to say *what more* than this they mean when they form the judgments expressed by such sentences; but I think it also true that they *intend* to mean something more, and believe that they do so. This belief may be illusory. Nevertheless, it occurs; and psychological analysis of the moral judgment which leaves this feature of it unmentioned is incomplete. The case is, of course, much the same with the ordinary aesthetic judgments; but, though some philosophers of aesthetics are zealous to maintain that in these too something more is meant than a report on the subjective hedonic reaction of the observer, the plain man, I suspect, does not think it so important to assert, when he calls a work of art 'beautiful,' that he means more than "I like it very much." But when, for example, with Mr. Churchill, he (the common man) calls the conduct of Adolf Hitler "wicked," if I am not mistaken, he does think it important to

assert that he means something more than "I am very unpleasantly affected when I think of it."

Hume, however, in the end does not reduce the meaning-
content of the moral judgment strictly to the assertion of an
individual affective reaction to the idea of one or another
motive or quality of character. For he believes that all men's
quasi-aesthetic reactions to the ideas of such motives or
qualities—their disinterested approbations and disapprobations—are, at any rate in the main, identical. Certain kinds
of actions, and the motives from which they are assumed to
arise, he thinks are approved by everybody; and this is
above all true of benevolence.

> In whatever light [he says], we take this subject, the
> merit ascribed to the social virtues appears still uniform,
> and arises chiefly from that regard which the natural
> sentiment of benevolence engages us to pay to the inter-
> ests of mankind and society. If we consider the principles
> of human make, such as they appear to daily experience
> and observation, we must, *a priori* conclude it to be
> impossible for such a creature as man to be totally indif-
> ferent to the well or ill-being of his fellow-creatures, and
> not readily, of himself, to pronounce where nothing gives
> him any particular bias, that what promotes their happi-
> ness is good, what tends to their misery is evil, without
> any farther regard or consideration.[2]

Hume's language here sounds rather like that of an intui-
tionist in ethical theory, one who holds that there are certain self-evident propositions about good and bad, certain

[2] *Enquiry Concerning the Principles of Morals*, Pt. II, Sec. 5;
Selby-Bigge, ed. p. 230.

moral axioms, the truth of which our reason recognizes; and
that our apprehension of their truth can, and should, of itself determine our choices. But that, of course, is not Hume's
real position. He is still simply propounding what he regards as an empirical generalization, or approximate generalization, about a species of state-of-things, the idea of the
realization of which arouses a present "satisfaction." Because of our susceptibility to pleasure from this idea, we
approve of acts, or motives, which tend to realize that state-
of-things, or disapprove the opposite, since 'approbation'
and 'disapprobation' are only other names for the feelings
of pleasure or uneasiness arising on the contemplation of
certain acts or motives. But since, as Hume believes, all men
—subject to some qualifications—react emotionally in the
same way when they contemplate (for example) "the well or
ill-being of their fellow creatures," a judgment of approbation may be said, for Hume also, to mean *something* more
than 'I am pleasantly affected when I view a certain kind of
action;' it means 'I and everybody else are so affected.' And
thus he conceives that moral judgments are not, as his doctrine might at first seem to imply, just expressions of the
personal and arbitrary likes and dislikes of individuals;
they have, or aim at, the kind of objectivity which consists
in conformity with the general consensus of mankind. When
a man

> bestows on any [other] man, the epithets of *vicious*, or
> *odious*, or *depraved*, he . . . expresses sentiments in which
> he *expects* all his audience are to concur with him. He
> must here, therefore, depart from his private and particu-
> lar situation, and must choose a point of view common to

him with others; he must move some universal principle
of the human frame, and touch a string to which all mankind have an accord and symphony."[3]

When you approve an action, or class of actions, then, you
are asserting one factual proposition, though it is a proposition *about* feelings or desires; namely, that people in general would, in "viewing" it, experience the same feeling or
desire that you do.

In thus asserting the universality and uniformity of the
approbations and disapprobations of all men, Hume was
obviously in error. Though he was right in saying men are
moved in their judgments of the conduct of others by their
feelings of approval and disapproval, it was not true that
the *kinds* of conduct approved or disapproved are the same
among all peoples and cultures; they have varied immensely
in the course of human history.

In all this, as I have said, Hume has simply been trying
to give an account of moral judgments, that is, of approbations and disapprobations, which will be consistent with the
fact that it is possible for them to function as *motives* determining the choice and action of the individual making
them. No account of them *would* be consistent with this fact
which represented them merely as the apprehensions of the
truth of propositions—at least, of propositions referring to
anything other than the affective states or the desires of that
individual and of other men. Yet to describe them in terms
consistent with their potential efficacy as motives does not

[3] *Enquiry Concerning the Principles of Morals*, Pt. I, Sec. 9;
Selby-Bigge, ed., p. 272.

really tell us their *modus operandi;* the detailed analysis of the actual processes of motivation in which approbation and disapprobation figure has still to be made. It is this analysis that constitutes the most original part of the doctrine of Hume and Adam Smith.

In this inquiry into the way in which the "moral sentiments" originate and operate in the individual who is moved by them, both Hume and Smith begin by considering the individual as an approver or disapprover, not as the object of approbation or disapprobation. They seek to show how his habit of passing judgments upon other men gives rise to motives which influence his own conduct. In order to show this they both employ, though Smith does it more clearly, what may be called the approbational triangle. In order to understand the phenomenon of approval or disapproval we must recognize that three persons, and not two, are involved in it. There is John, the spectator, who is approving or disapproving; there is James, the agent, whose acts or motives are to be the subjects of John's approval or disapproval; but there is also Thomas, who is, so to say, the patient or victim, the third person, on whom James is acting, or who is affected by his acts. Thomas may, of course, represent a multitude of persons.

Now, there is in John a propensity to sympathize with Thomas. "Sympathy," in the terminology of Hume and Smith, does not mean, though it includes, pity or kindly feeling; it is the tendency which they believe to be universal in man, to receive by communication the feelings and inclinations and, indeed, also the opinions of others, when no interest of one's own intervenes to prevent. "This propensity makes us enter deeply into each other's sentiments, and causes like passions to run, as it were by contagion," from one individual to another. John, then, tends to share Thomas' emotional reactions to what James does to him (Thomas). If James's acts cause pain to Thomas, John will feel pain, though doubtless in a weaker degree; and he will in some degree share Thomas' feeling towards James—anger, indignation, hatred. These attitudes towards James which John acquires by sympathy with Thomas, the victim, constitute John's disapprovals, or approvals, of James; he disapproves those acts of James (or the motives which he believes to inspire them) that produce a vicarious feeling of pain in himself. When John approves of James he sympathizes with, "enters into," *his* "sentiments" and regards them with satisfaction on the basis of his own participation in the sentiments produced in Thomas by James's behavior. These reactions on John's part towards Thomas and James, it is true, vary widely under differing circumstances; it is in distinguishing their variations and the conditions which limit or modify John's ability to sympathize with, and reproduce, Thomas' attitudes towards James that Adam Smith is especially ingenious and penetrating.

But into these minutiae we cannot enter. The general point is that, in deriving approbation or its opposite from sympathy with a third party or parties, Hume and Smith find reason for concluding that approbational judgments are essentially disinterested and impersonal, not merely expressions either of John's own desires or of his private opinions, and also that they are, in their broad features, uniform. For Thomas will never be pleased at being injured by

James; and *in so far as* John's judgments of James are a reflection of Thomas', they will be equally invariable.

Such judgments, moreover, naturally take on a generalized form. John does not in each separate instance go through the process of "entering into the sentiments" of a particular Thomas or James; it becomes habitual with him to approve certain *kinds* of acts and disapprove others, to feel pleasure or displeasure at the "view" of them.

When John has thus become habituated to passing judgments of approval or disapproval, praise or blame, upon the acts or assumed motives of James and everybody else, it is impossible that he should not pass similiar judgments upon his own acts, or those to which he may feel an inclination. John, who at first played the role merely of critical spectator, now becomes *both* critical spectator and agent. When he does so, what determines his judgments of his own acts, actual or prospective? What are the laws of *self*-approval or disapproval? The simplest answer would be that John as spectator tends to apply to himself as agent the judgments which he is accustomed to apply to James—or the whole tribe of Jameses, that is, of agents—under similar circumstances; and this simple answer, I think, is in general correct, as was previously intimated when I spoke of the boomerang-effect of the approbation of others.

But this is not, for Hume and Smith, the whole story— though this point is developed more clearly and fully by Smith. When John was judging James, in the light of the James-Thomas situation, he was acting as an *impartial* spectator. He himself was outside of that situation, in the sense that his private interests were not involved and that he had no initial bias as between James and Thomas. Now, says Smith in substance, when John turns to judging himself, he is aware that his judgment must be such as would be made upon him by a spectator in the same situation in which *he* originally was vis-à-vis James and Thomas, that is, by a detached spectator.

> We can never [Smith declares] survey our own sentiments and motives, we can never form any judgment concerning them, unless we remove ourselves, as it were, from our own natural station, and endeavor to view them as at a certain distance from us. But we can do this in no other way than by endeavouring to view them with the eyes of other people, or as other people are likely to view them. Whatever judgment we can form concerning them, accordingly, must always bear some secret reference, either to what are, or to what, upon a certain condition, would be, or what we imagine ought to be, the judgment of others. We endeavour to examine our own conduct as we imagine any other fair and impartial spectator would view it. If, upon placing ourselves in his situation, we thoroughly enter into all the passions and motives which influence it, we approve of it by sympathy with the approbation of this supposed equitable judge. If otherwise, we enter into his disapprobation, and condemn it.[4]

In short, when we take a favorable or an unfavorable view of an act or motive of our own, we implicitly assert a claim that any distinterested observer, fully acquainted with the facts and constituted as human beings *are* generally con-

[4] *Theory of Moral Sentiments*, Pt. III, ch. 1, p. 99.

stituted, would *feel* the same way about that act or motive; and if we have any doubt about this, we feel an uneasy suspicion of our self-judgment. There is thus created a sort of social situation inside the individual; he has, as it were, admitted another man within his breast, to sit in judgment upon him, and with whom he engages in a sort of internal debate. The man within John's breast is, it is true, a construct in John's imagination; but he cannot be constructed just as John fancies; on the contrary, he is often a very independent and annoying fellow. And since he is the hypothetical internal spokesman of the judgments of any *actual* disinterested spectator, John's impressions as to what this inner critic *would* say can, and by implication should, be checked, by comparison with what actual spectators, so far as they can be presumed to be informed and disinterested, *do* say about the kind of acts or motives which characterize John's actual or contemplated conduct.

All this—allowing for a certain figurativeness in the expression of it—appears to me to be a correct description of an aspect of ordinary moral experience. But it does not, so far, seem to explain how John's judgments of himself *motivate* his action. It tells us that these *judgments* must be in accord with those which he passes upon other people, but it does not show us how *desires* come to be connected with them. To this question, two different answers can, I think, be distinguished in Hume and Smith. According to the first, which is to be found in some passages of Hume, the answer is already implicit in the foregoing analysis. John has been shown to find pleasure or displeasure in the "view" of certain actions, characteristics, or motives of James, when they are considered in the light of the emotional reactions of the person or persons whom they affect. This association of pleasant or unpleasant feeling with the ideas of such acts becomes *fixed* in John's mind; and therefore, when he thinks of himself as performing similar acts, he is pleased or displeased with himself; which is another way of saying that he feels a desire to act in the way that he habitually approves in other people and an aversion from acting in the way that he disapproves. Here what we have called the desire of self-esteem is a direct derivative from the propensity to pass judgments of approbation, or the contrary, upon others.

According to the other answer, which is also suggested by Hume, but is more evident in Smith, the desire of self-esteem seems to be a derivative from approbativeness—the "love of praise" is Smith's name for it. While we begin by passing "moral criticisms upon the characters and conduct of other people, . . . we soon learn that they are equally frank with regard to our own." And it is in these approbations or disapprobations of a man by others that "he *first* views the propriety and impropriety of his own passions, the beauty and deformity of his own mind." This gives rise to a new "passion"; he *wants* to be approved, or not to be disapproved; "he will be elevated in the one case, and cast down in the other." But though approbativeness is (apparently) regarded by Smith as genetically prior, it is not for him the ultimate and decisive determinant of moral behavior—that is, of behavior influenced by moral judgments. For after we discover that, and how, other people actually judge of us, "we become anxious to know whether we *deserve* their censure or applause." We do not accept their judgments as necessarily final, and accordingly we—in the manner previously indicated—"suppose ourselves to be spectators [external examiners, so to say] of our own behavior, and imagine what effect it would, in this light, produce upon us. . . . If this view pleases us, we are tolerably satisfied."[5] Here a desire distinct from the simple "love of praise" emerges; the "love of praiseworthiness," the wish to be the kind of person who is *entitled* to the approval of a genuinely competent and impartial spectator, and it is the love of praiseworthiness that is, for Smith, the distinctively moral motive. *It* is a desire to *be* and not merely to appear. Yet what is desired is still, you observe, the possibility of believing that one's qualities or acts are the legitimate subjects of adjectives expressing favorable attitudes on the part of a hypothetical ideal observer and critic. In the end this last conception, by Smith, as by Milton long before him, is identified with the conception of God; for both, the moral consciousness finds its completion in the religious consciousness. This conclusion, however, was rather an expression of religious piety than any implication drawn from the psychological analysis of purely moral phenomena and therefore does not fall within the province of this lecture.

[5] *Ibid.*, Pt. II, ch. 1, p. 101.

Index ❧ ❧ ❧

A

Abbadie, Jacques, on rationalization, 29–31; compared with D. Hume, 30–31; on the reason, 30–31; his views of pride, 133; reduces the passions to *laudum cupido*, 143; on pride as distinctively human, 146; on the desire for fame and glory as implanted by the Creator, 160–163; his scorn of approbativeness, 235–236

Adams, James Luther, 9n

Adams, John, on self-deceit or rationalization, 32–34; on the importance of emulative approbativeness, 197 f.; the irrational character of the passion for distinction, 199–200; vanity as implanted by Nature, 200; three varieties of passion for distinction, 200–201; desire for approbation contrasted with Benevolence, 202–203; on the political superiority of the Romans, 203; his views contrasted with those of Montesquieu, 203n; relation to Thomas Jefferson, 204n; on hereditary aristocracies, 206–207

Addison, Joseph, reaction to denigration of man, 19

Amour-propre, 99, 235

Anti-intellectualism and anti-scientism, 221 f.; in Milton,; 223; in Rousseau, 222, 224–227; in Seneca, 222; in Voltaire, 224

Approbational judgments, as disinterested and impersonal, in Hume, 250 f., 259; in Adam Smith, 259 f.; their universality and uniformity, according to Hume, 256–257

Approbational triangle, in Hume and Adam Smith, 258 f.

Approbativeness, definition of, 88 f.; 130-192 *passim*; its peculiarity as a biological phenomenon, 91; the differentia of man *par excellence*, 92-93; relation to approbations and disapprobations, 93 f.; approbation or disapprobation of the approbational attitude in general, 94 f.; 129, 195, 207; (*see* Pride)

Aristotle, on magnanimity, 96–97; on honor, 96-97; his conception of God adopted by the Christians, 160

Augustine, 3

Aversion, definition of, 71

B

Bayle, 16n

Becker, Carl, 53

Behaviorism, 91 f.

Bentley, Eric, 14

Bidney, David A., 239n

Blackmore, Sir Richard, on the value of the desire for glory, 164

Boas, G., 4n; 16n; 222n

Boileau, 15, 19; and the scorn of approbativeness, 235

Boomerang-effect, of approbations and disapprobations, 103, 117

Brant, Irving, 47n, 48n, 55n

Brooke, Henry, 16

Brutus, Abbadie on, 143

Burke, Edmund, on pride as distinctive of man, 148-150

Butler, Bishop, on approbativeness as nonrational and egoistic, but beneficent, 179-180

C

Cary, 156n

Censorious people, 95 f.

Christianity, rejection of approbativeness, 98

Cicero, on glory, 156

Clutton-Brock, A., on pooled self-esteem, 117 ff.

Compensations, 100

Consistency in judging, 103 f.

Constitution, American, 38, 47, 53-55, 63

Constitutional Convention, 46

Continental Congress of 1776, 46

Counterpoise, the method of, 39-40; Hooker on, 40-41; Madison on, 48 ff.; Mandeville on, 41; Morris on 57-60, 63; Pascal on, 40; Pope on, 42-45, 169-170; Vauvenargues on, 45-46; Voltaire on, 39; William Whitehead on, 45

Cynics, 101

D

Dante, on the love of fame and honor, 156

Davila, Henrico Caterino, 198

Deliberate choice, analysis of, 70 f.

Delusions of grandeur, 100

Descartes, 39

Deshoulières, Mme., 16

Desire, definition of, 70 f.; 74

Diogenes, 101

Disapprobation of approbativeness as such, cause of, 234 f. the discovery of the irrational, Max Lerner on, 22

Dishonor, the fear of, 164–165

Disinterested desires, 86

Drives, 74

Dyke, Daniel, 26

E

Earl of Rochester, 16

Economics, place of emulative approbativeness in, 208 ff.

Edman, I., 108

Edwards, Jonathan, 3; on the greatest good, 77–78

Effects of pride, Burke on, 221; Mandeville on, 220–221; Voltaire on, 221; Young on, 220–221

Ego, 11

Egoism, 84 f.

Elliot, 58n

Emerson, R. W., 6

Emulativeness, or the desire for superiority, 112 f.; Alfred Adler on, 112; Hobbes on, 113–114, 116; W. S. Gilbert on, 113–114; John Adams on, 204–205; its role in acquisition of wealth, 213–215; Adam Smith on, 213 f.; T. Veblen on, 213 f.

Esprit, Jacques, 26–28; on pride as the source of humility, 155

Ethical inwardness, in the appraisal of pride, 153

Ethics, Christian, 9; of Hume, 247 ff.; of Adam Smith, 247 ff.; two classes of phenomena pertinent to, 247–248

Euripides, on the desire for fame, 97n

F

Factions, Madison on, 47–48, 52, 57

Fame, as denoting both a desire and the object of a desire, 130; the desire for implanted by God, 158–170

Fawkes, Francis, 16

Federalist, 46, 58; Number 10, 41–52, 54; Number 51, 55

Fowler, O. S. and L. N., 90n

Freud, 11

Fureur de se distinguer, in Rousseau, 149–151

G

Gandhi, 113

Gay, 16

Gloriae cupiditas, in Mariana, 131–132

Gloriae studium, in Mariana, 158

Glory, the quest of, in Pascal, 132

God, as the implanter of the desire for fame and praise, 158–170

Goldring, Arthur, 5

Goldsmith, 16

Gould, Robert, 16, 17

Greeks and Romans, approval of approbativeness, 96 f.

Greville, Robert, his use of "fame" and "honour," 130

H

Halifax, Lord, 32; reduces all the passions to pride, 142–143

Hamilton, Alexander, 55n

Hamlet, 34, 108

Harvey, H. Brampton, 32n

Hedonic parasitism, 219; in Boileau, 230; in La Placette, 229–230; in Lucretius, 228–229; in Pascal, 229; in Rousseau, 230–231

Hedonic susceptibility, 70 f.; 248

Helvetius, 45–46

Henderson, L. J., 243

Hero, D. Wecter on, 14; E. Bentley on, 14; S. Hook on, 14

Heroes, 94; taste in, 13

History of the idea of man, 13 f.

Hobbes, Thomas, on emulative approbativeness, 113–114, 118; on the passion of glory as distinctively human, 145–146

Hocking, W. E., 108

Homo homine lupus, in Plautus, Pliny and Juvenal, 4

Homo sapiens, as inferior to other animals, 16

Honour, as denoting both a desire and the object of a desire, 130; love of, implanted by God, 158–170

Hook, Sidney, 14

Hooker, 40–41

Hume, David, 181–190 and 247 ff.; compared with Abbadie, 30–31; on the inability of the reason to oppose the passions, 181 f.; on the inability of the reason to be a motive to action, 181 f.; on the instrumental use of the understanding, 182; on passions and desires, 182–183;

on approbativeness, 181 f.; on self-esteem, 181 f.; moral sentiments in, 184; close kinship of approbativeness and virtue, 185–186; the principle of comparison, 188; his relation to Mandeville, 188–190; on the origin of moral sentiments, 258 f.; ethics of, 247 ff.; moral judgments in, 247; how desires are associated with moral judgments, 262–264

Humility, as a form of self-esteem and pride, 154 f.

I

"I" and "Me," 81 f.

Id, 11

Ideas of states-of-things, 71 f., 75-77

Indictment of pride, 217 ff.; specific counts in indictment, 219

J

James, William, 107; on first personal pronoun, 83

Jenyns, Soame, 32

Jeremiah, 2

Johnson, Samuel, on pride and the love of praise, 137–138

Judgments, aesthetic, compared with moral, 251–253

Juvenal, 4

K

Kant, I., on approbativeness, 193; compared with Mandeville, 192

Kaye, 26*n*, 170

L

La Bruyère, on vanity and praise, 143–144; on vanity, 237; 16, 31

Lachèvre, F., 17*n*

l'amour de soi, 147–148

l'amour, propre, 148

La Placette, J., 28–29, 210–211; on pride, 133–134; on pride as distinctively human, 146; on humility as a source of pride, 154–155

La Rouchefoucauld, 16, 18, 20, 31, 40

laudis studium, in Mariana, 157

laudum cupido, 143

Law, William, on Mandeville, 178; on the intrinsic evil of pride, 241–243

Lerner, Max, 22–23

Love of fame, 130; in Edward Young, 137–140; *see* Pride, Approbativeness

Love of praise, 136 ff.; in Abbadie, 143; in La Bruyère, 144; in La Placette, 146; 158–192 *passim*; see Pride, Approbativeness

Love of praiseworthiness, in Adam Smith, 263–264

Lucretius, on hedonic parasitism, 228–229

M

Machiavelli, 16

Madison, James, on "factions," 47–49; on the method of counterpoise, 48 ff.; 59*n*, 60, 62*n*, 205

Malebranche, on rationalization, 26; on pride and vanity, 132–133

Man, as both actor and spectator, 106–107

Man, as inferior to beasts, 16 f.; Mme. Deshoulières on, 16; Swift on, 17; Johnson on, 17

Mandeville, Bernard de, on the method of counterpoise, 41; 42*n*; on private vices and public benefits, 170 f.; on pride as the vice from which most benefits flow, 171; on human morality as a result of pride, 171 f.; on approbativeness and self-esteem, 171 f.; on the Lawgivers, 172; Mandeville and Rousseau, 173, 224; on emulation, 174; on man's reasonableness, 176; on pride in children, 177; Law's criticism of Mandeville, 178–179; Mandeville and Abbadie, 179; and Voltaire, 180–181; and Hume, 188–190; on the dependence of the pursuit of wealth on pride, 211; appraisal of the desire for possessions, 212

Man's general badness, 1 ff. J. Edwards on, 3–4; Juvenal on, 4; R. Niebuhr on, 8;

Philip of Mornay on, 5; Pliny and Plautus on, 4; Voltaire on, 5–6; the reaction to assertion of man's badness, by Addison and Vauvenargues, 19–21

Man's natural goodness, 7

Mariana, on *gloriae cupiditas*, 131–132; on the desire of glory as distinctively human, 145; on the value of the desire for praise, 157–158

McDougall, William, 10–11, 107

Melmoth, William the younger, on the value of the love of praise, 168

Method in historiography, 67–69

Mill, John Stuart, 78

Milton, John, his use of "fame" in *Lycidas*, 130, 158; on the value of the desire for praise, 158–160; compared with Adam Smith, 264; and anti-scientism, 223

Mind-body problem, 72 f.

Montesquieu, 39*n*, 195

Moral choice, motivation of, 247 f.

Moral judgments, 247 f.; Hume on, 247; how desires are associated with them, according to Hume and Adam Smith, 262–264; moral judgments compared with aesthetic judgments, 251 f.

Moral sentiments, in Hume, 184–185; on the origin of moral sentiments, in Hume and Smith, 258 f.

Mores, 94

Morris, Gouveneur, on the Senate, 57 ff.; on the method of counterpoise, 57–60

Motive, definition of, 71

N

National anthems, outbursts of collective self-glorification, 118

Natural rights, 46

Niebuhr, R., on the reality of evil, 8

O

Oldham, 16

Original sin, doctrine of, 2 f.; J. Edwards on, 3

Other consciousness, 84–87

P

Pareto, 23

Pascal, 18; on rationalization, 29; on the method of counterpoise, 40; on the quest of glory, 132; his scorn of approbativeness, 234, 236; on pride, 239–241; on pride as a motive in education, 244

Passion of glory, 130; as distinctively human, 145

Passions, 70, 129; reduced to pride, 141–144

Philauty, 99

Philip of Mornay, 5

Plato, 101

Plautus, 4

Pliny, 4

Pooled self-esteem, 117 ff.; A. Clutton-Brock on, 117 ff.

Pope, Alexander, 16; on statecraft, 42 f.; on the method of counterpoise, 42 f.; on man's irrationality, 42–45; on self-love, 43; on the passions as the sole determinant of conduct, 43–44; on the "master passion," 43; on the social utility of the love of praise, 169–170; 64

Port Royal, school at, 244

Pride, as man's chief folly, 2; as a motive in education, 241–245; on the indictment of pride, 217 ff.; 130; as the most powerful of human motives, 131; in Malebranche, 132–133; in Jacques Abbadie, 133; in Jacques La Placette, 133–134; negative and positive aspects of, in John Locke, 134–136; in Dr. Johnson, 137–138; in Edward Young, 137–140; in Cuthbert Shaw, 140; all other passions reduced to, 141–144; as the psychic differentia of man, 144–151; as the dynamic of good conduct, 153–192; the favorable appraisal of pride, 218–219; pride as a substitute for reason and virtue, 151 ff.; *See* Approbativeness,

Self-esteem, Emulativeness, Love of praise

Primary needs, 220

Primitivism, 220, 222 f.

Primitivists, compared with Mandeville, 171

Psychological hedonism, 70 ff.

Psychology, as a discipline, 10

Psychopathology, 11

Q

Quakers, 113

Quest of honor, 130; *see* Honour

R

Rationalization, recognition of in the seventeenth and eighteenth centuries, 24 f.; Daniel Dyke on, 25–26; Jacques Esprit on, 26–28; La Placette on, 28–29; Malebranche on, 26; Pascal on, 29; Jacques Abbadie on, 29–31; La Rochefoucauld on, 31; La Bruyère on, 31; Lord Halifax on, 32; Soame Jenyns on, 32; John Adams on, 32–34

Ray, John, on the fear of dishonor as implanted by God, 164–165

Reason, in Abbadie, 30–31; in Hume, 181 ff.; in Pope, 42–45; the love of praise as a substitute for, 153–192 *pas-*

sim; *See* Rationalization and Anti-intellectualism

Romans, reasons for political superiority of, 203

Rousseau, and anti-intellectualism, 222; on the indictment of pride, 222 ff.; on hedonic parasitism, 230–233; on science of ethnology, 231–232; and primitivism, 232*n*; on the intrinsic evil of pride, 243–244; and Mandeville, 173, 224; on the significance of approbativeness for legislation, 197; on pride as the source of the desire for wealth, 213; on *l'orgueil* and *l'amour de soi*, 146–148; on pride in the development of civilization, 149–151

Russell, Lord, 124

S

Santayana, 108; on consciousness, 73

Self, analysis of, 81 f.; genesis of, 84 f.; genesis of, according to Clifford, Royce, Baldwin, 85; Hegel, on the genesis of, 86

Self-abasement, 2

Self-appraisal, 102

Self-approbativeness, relation to morality, 105 f.

Self-consciousness, 107; results in self-division, 106; how it affects desire and choice, 81 f.

Self-deception, 24 f.; *See* Rationalization

Self-distrust, 1 f.

Self-esteem, desire for, 99 f.; relation to approbativeness, 100 f.; proposal to eliminate it, by Clufton-Brock, 125–126; craving for or aversion from self-disesteem, as a biological singularity, 105; 129, 195, *passim*; *see* Pride, Approbativeness

Self-sufficiency, 101

Seneca, and anti-intellectualism, 222

Sermon on the Mount, its repudiation by Mariana, 158

Shakespeare, W., 206

Shaw, Cuthbert, on pride and love of fame, 140

Shenstone, 16

Sidney, Sir Phillip, 5

Sloan, Eugene H., 17*n*.

Smith, Adam, 112; on approbativeness, 190–191; recognizes both negative and positive aspects of approbativeness, 190; impartial spectator, 191, 260–262; role of approbativeness in education, 191–192; emulation as the motive for the acquisition of wealth, 213–215; compared with Veblen, 213–215; on how the moral sentiments operate, 258 f.; sympathy in Smith, 258; ethics of, 247 ff.; the love of praiseworthiness, 264; analysis of moral judg-

ments, 262–264; the appro-
bational triangle, 258 f.;
compared with Milton, 264
Socrates, 77
Soviet Union, 123
Spinoza, on pride, 238–239
Stoicism, 101, 113, 228
Superego, 12
Swift, 16, 17
Sympathy, in Hume and Adam
Smith, 258–259

T

Terminal and adjectival values,
79 f.
Terminology, 129 f.
Time, significance of, in voluntary choice, 76 f.
Troland, Leonard, 10; and
hedonism of the present, 78

U

United States, 123; Constitution
of, 204–205

V

Values, adjectival and terminal,
99–100, 248 ff.
Vanity, in Pascal, 132; in Malebranche, 132–133; in La
Bruyère, 143–144; *see* Pride
Vauvenargues, on man's disgrace, 37; on private and
public interest, 45; reaction
to denigration of man, 19–21;

on the value of the love of
praise, 167–168
Veblen, Thorstein, on the psychological inquiry into the
principal motives of the acquisition and expenditure of
wealth, 208 ff.; 220
Vergil, 151
Verneuil, Jean, 31n
Vice, as the parent of virtue, in
Mandeville, 171–172
Victims of the Inquisition, 80
Victorian Era, 7
Voltaire, on the general badness
of man, 5–6; on the method
of counterpoise, 39; on anti-
intellectualism, 224; on the
social value of pride, 180–181

W

Wecter, Dixon, 14
Westminster Catechism, 3
Whitehead, William, 45
Whitehorn, Dr. John C., on the
"desire for goals," and the
"desire for roles," 80n
Wolff, Christian, on the value
of glory and fame, 107

Y

Young, Edward, on pride and
love of fame, 137–140; the
love of fame as a gift of
heaven, 165–167; on the economic effects of pride, 211–
212; on pride, 236–237